The Science of Violin Playing

by

RAPHAEL BRONSTEIN

Paganiniana Publications, Inc.

211 West Sylvania Ave., Neptune, New Jersey 07753

TABLE OF CONTENTS

ISBN 0-87666-601-2

SCIENCE OF VIOLIN PLAYING

Chapter One
PRINCIPLES OF VISUAL INTONATION

INTRODUCTION

Of all the technical obstacles facing a string player when he takes up his instrument to create music the most ever-present problem, and certainly the most obvious to both listener and performer, is that of intonation. It is the greatest source of anxiety to a player regardless of what level of proficiency or professionalism he has attained. Faulty intonation is a plague which might strike in very difficult technical passages or in the most simple melodies. It is like a disease which afflicts all levels of society regardless of social or economic class. During my many years of experience as a pedagogue I have developed a system by examining the mistakes of many students which can serve as a guide to overcoming this obstacle. It is not a panacea but it is surely a most innovative step in the development of the techniques for teaching the violin. I call it the study of "visual intonation."

The system of practicing intonation in the old school of playing, and one which is still widely used today, was repetition; a constant replaying of an interval until it was "set" in the hand—until it had become second nature; somewhat like a baby learning to walk one step at a time. This system of course took many hours of hard work over many years, and even then there was no guarantee that under the slightest strain or pressure, or when there was a break in the routine of practicing, it wouldn't falter. Exceptional cases of course did and do exist in the greatest artists, but those were the chosen few who were gifted with a natural instinct for true intonation.

This new system, created for the vast majority of violinists (and theoretically for all string players) who are not so gifted is designed to save many hours of practice. It is based not on chance as was the old school, but on knowledge of the physical (muscular) and psychological problems involved in playing. The "truth" of intonation is judged by hearing, but that of course is after the fact—the note has already been played out of tune. My concept is based on visualizing intellectually (knowing beforehand) the spaces or distances between notes with the various fingers so that each note can be created with a "before the fact" knowledge. This means that a distance between notes, whether large or small must be visualized and diagnosed. There must be a conscious effort to "aim" for the next note before placing the fingers.

This does not exclude using aural guidance to judge intonation. The player must certainly sing the notes to himself as he plays, but the real truth of intonation is a combination of using this aural faculty and analyzing scientifically the distances from one note (or finger) to the next. These spaces must be secured both in our mind and hand *through slow practice*. Only after this is achieved should the student attempt to play passages up to tempo.

Specific examples are given throughout the following text, but I have listed below some general exercises which when practiced with all the following principles in mind will develop a secure knowledge of the fingerboard.

SCHRADIECK Book 1

II — the whole exercise
VIII — #1-7
X — #4-8
XI — #15-16
XIII — the whole exercise especially #6
XVII — the whole exercise, especially #9-11
XX — #9-14

SEVCIK Opus 1 Part III

#1, 3, 5, 6—should be practiced by taking one line of each at one time
#7 — especially the diminished arpeggios
#II — as is
#12 — skip the three lines with trills

SEVCIK Opus 1 Part IV

#2, 6, 11—should be practiced a line of each at one time, then study the rest of the book

The principles of visual intonation are divided into two basic sections: the first involves single notes and the second concerns double-stops. It should be noted, however, that when a passage of single notes involves string crossings—as in the Dont, Op. 35 #7—it must be treated as double-stops and employ those those principles.

PRINCIPLES OF SINGLE NOTES

To create the most comfortable position visualize the left hand as encompassing a perfect fourth between the 1st and 4th fingers.

There is a natural tendency to place the hand close to the head of the violin in first position; however, the first basic principle of visual intonation is that a perfect fourth between the 1st and 4th fingers is a *small* distance. Create a comfortable feeling of compactness in the hand by moving "forward," almost to second position. Then each succeeding position must be farther forward so that the basic interval of the perfect fourth remains a small comfortable distance. The fingers should be placed more on the fleshy pad than the tip and the thumb should lie opposite either the 1st or 2nd finger, however it should never be farther back than the first finger.

When playing B-C on the A string:

the space between the first and second fingers is small, but there is some space, the fingers should not be touching. In half position when playing A sharp-B, which again is a half step between the 1st and 2nd fingers,

one might reason that because it is a lower position there is more distance between the fingers. In this case the reasoning does not hold true because when moving back to play these notes the thumb stays in first position and so creates an abnormally cramped feeling in the hand. The second finger must be placed lower than expected to counteract the pull on the hand by the thumb.

In general distances when descending should be felt slightly larger than when ascending because when ascending the lower fingers for the previous notes are already down to serve as a firm foundation. When descending the lower fingers are raised so there is no foundation on which to judge the distances.

2

When playing fifths, the notes A-E-B-F sharp each on successively higher strings:

as indicated in the example with the first finger, the finger must go back a little on each higher string because the joint in the finger narrows as you ascend. In second and third position it narrows less, so the finger should move back less. In the fourth position the distances are even across the strings, and in fifth position the first finger must move forward because the thumb, when locked in the neck presents an obstacle to the rest of the hand.

3

The spacial relationships between the fingers in any one position on one string fall into a basic pattern: for whole steps between the 1st and 2nd finger is a large distance, between 2nd and 3rd is more normal, from 3rd to 4th finger is a small distance. For example on the A string:

this can be understood clearly if you remember that in each successively higher position a specific distance (in this case the whole step) gets smaller and smaller. Here the whole step between each next two higher fingers represents the next higher position. There is a psychological, an anxiety element, which can cause the second finger to over-extend because of the anticipation of the D sharp and E sharp—this aspect of intonation will be discussed more fully later.

When moving a half step with the same finger the distance must be felt larger than anticipated because each half step is equal to the width of the tip of the finger and so must be compensated for.

Consider the chromatic scale from B to E on the A string.

Between the 1st and 2nd finger (B to C) a half step in first position is *not* tight, from C natural to C sharp is a larger distance than might be thought because of the width of the finger, from 2nd to 3rd finger (C sharp to D) is a small distance, D to D sharp is played with the same finger and so is a larger distance, and from 3rd to 4th finger a half step is very small so D sharp to E must be very tight (use less flesh with the 4th finger). In general when playing in the higher positions the distances are smaller so less flesh (played more with the tip of the finger) must be used.

Here as with the whole step pattern when descending all distances must be felt larger than ascending; so from 4th to 3rd finger (E to D sharp) is a larger distance than 3rd to 4th finger, as noted by the brackets in the example, and so on down the scale: D sharp to D is a large distance because the same finger is used, D to C sharp is not very close, and C to B is not close.

In scale work from the fifth position on up the thumb is not parallel to the 1st finger so to compensate the distances between 1st and 2nd finger must be felt larger. With each higher position the web between the thumb and the hand becomes more stretched and so the resistance becomes greater and must be compensated for. The distances between 2nd and 3rd, and 3rd and 4th fingers however, become smaller.

4

One of the basic principles of visual intonation is that each note must be created in relation to what was played before. It follows therefore that the notes preceding any particular note will have an effect on the placement of the finger for that note. If for example you play:

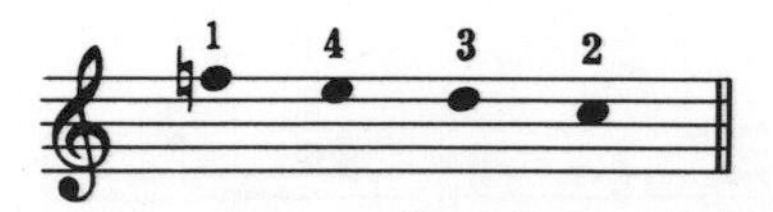

the natural tendency will be to play the D flatter than it should be because the 1st finger on the F will pull the hand out of shape (out of the natural perfect fourth configuration between the 1st and 4th fingers). To compensate for this the 3rd finger on D must be placed closer to the 4th finger and the 2nd must also be higher.

In the reverse direction:

the G will have a tendency to be pulled sharp by the 4th finger so it must be played closer to the 1st, and the 3rd finger on A must be lower.

Another example where this principle of the influence of preceding notes is important is:

Here the general rule is that when there is a half step between 1st and 2nd finger, a whole step between 2nd and 3rd finger must be felt smaller than usual because after playing a half step there is a tendency to exaggerate the larger whole step.

An excellent example to use in the study of the influence of preceding notes is Kreutzer étude #12. When practicing this exercise you should remember that when a finger is skipped as between 1st and 3rd, or 2nd and 4th two tones-as C to E is a large distance and one and a half tones-as C to E flat is small. The basic rules for this exercise are that when the distance between the 1st and 3rd fingers is small the space from 3rd to 4th is large; conversely when 1st to 3rd is large, 3rd to 4th is very small. In measure 2 of Kreutzer #12 the notes are:

Of the last three notes C to E is two tones but should be played small because of the psychological influence of the next stretch from E to A with the 3rd and 4th fingers.

In the next example (measure #16),

the 1st finger on B is in the fourth position, the 3rd finger on E is an extension so from E to G sharp (3rd to 4th finger) is a small distance. In measure 22,

From C to E is a small distance because E to A with the 3rd and 4th fingers is a large distance, from E to A with the 1st and 3rd finger is large and A to C with the 3rd and 4th fingers is small.

When changing position on the same note, to play with a different finger, the distance should be felt small.

When moving to the next position do so with the hand, think in small distances and don't reach with the finger.

6

When crossing strings with the same finger to a note which is not a parallel note such as:

the distance is larger than anticipated because of the space between the strings and the opening up of the joint of the finger, even though C to C sharp is a half step with the same finger,

and as such is a large distance.

In the following example the marking ⁄\ indicates where these cases occur:

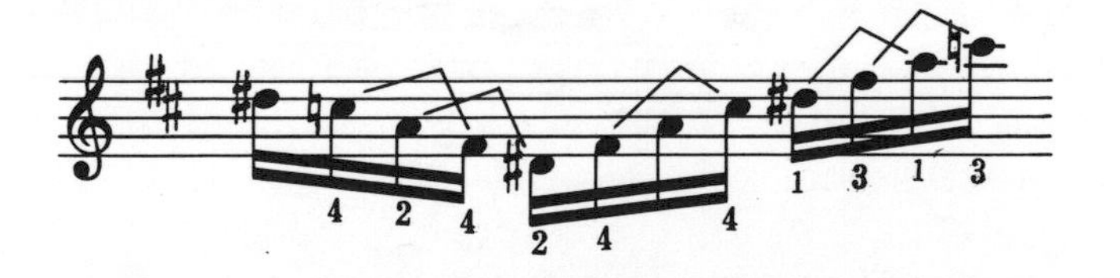

as in going from C to F sharp with the 4th finger, or from D sharp to A with the 1st finger.

7

In shifting from one note to another think of the motion between the two notes as building a bridge. Before moving the finger, hand, or arm get a mental image of where the next note lies on the fingerboard, then *aim* for that note. Essentially every shift is initiated from the elbow, the wrist line firm. Most importantly, you must have a visual picture of the distance to the next note, whether it is large or small; without a target there is nothing to aim at. There are two very useful exercises to use in developing this technique: Sevcik Op. 1, Part III, #11; and Dont Op. 35, #20. For example in the first measure of the Dont:

Hold the E and aim for the B with the 3rd finger already visualizing that the following G sharp is a small distance from B. In measure 2 of the same exercise.

hold the A and aim for the C#, measuring the distance between these notes. In measure 10:

Hold the B and aim for the D sharp, measuring the distance between these notes.

8

It is very useful in developing both the ear and the spacial feeling in the left hand to practice diminished arpeggios. An excellent exercise to practice is Sevcik Op.1 part III #10. Be aware that a minor third (1½ steps) between the 1st and 2nd finger is very large, between 1st and 3rd finger is small, and between 3rd and 4th is very large. Also, remember, as was already mentioned that all descending distances are larger than the same interval ascending.

9

When playing melodies of difficult intervals in the high positions it can be very helpful to practice them first in the lower positions an octave or two down, just to get the sound into the ear; as for example the runs on the last page of the Chausson Poème.

10

When playing scales ascending with the 1st and 2nd fingers, as:

All the distances must be carefully calculated. There is a tendency to take the whole steps for granted, but special care must be taken to visualize the half steps. After the thumb becomes locked in the neck the movement of the first finger must be exaggerated ascending and the second finger spaces are smaller. On the way down don't allow the thumb to pull the hand back too fast or far.

This same problem with the thumb will affect all large shifts to the higher positions. Compensation must be made for the resistance of the thumb when it locks in the neck.

11

To play fingered harmonics in tune the 1st finger should be placed a little sharp because a harmonic is by nature slightly flat. The 4th finger should be placed with the fleshy pad on the string.

PRINCIPLES OF DOUBLE-STOPS

1

When playing two notes as a double-stop aim for the lower finger and add the top finger; for example when playing a third with the 1st and 3rd fingers aim for the 1st and add the 3rd. In playing a three-note chord aim first for the middle note of the chord and set the other two in relation to it; in four-note chords aim first for the third note in the chord. It is generally a good idea to practice double-stops as broken intervals at first to get a good visual picture of the spacial relationships. This helps to create a greater feeling of security in playing the double-stops.

2

Thirds When playing a sequence of thirds don't raise the 1st and 3rd fingers when placing the 2nd and 4th. This will help to create a clearer picture of the spacial relationships between the fingers. If you play a major third such as B flat-D on the A string:

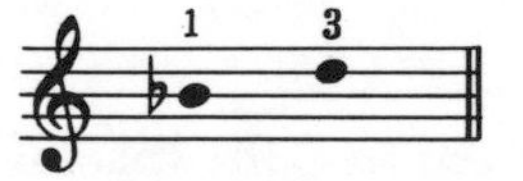

it is a large distance, two whole tones. When played on the D and A strings as a double-stop:

the relationship is the same as from D to F natural on the A string:

which is a small distance—one and a half tones, so we consider two tones (a major third) as a small distance when played as a third.

A minor third such as B-D on the A string:

is a small distance—one and a half tones. When played as a double-stop on the D and the A strings:

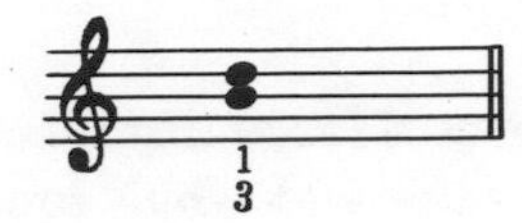

the parallel relationship on the A string is from D to F sharp:

or two whole tones which is a large distance. So we consider one and half tones (a minor third) as a large distance when played as a double-stopped third.

When playing any two thirds which employ whole steps between the 1st and 2nd fingers and 3rd and 4th fingers (playing from one major third to another), the distance between the 1st and second finger is large and the 3rd and 4th finger is small; as in the case with C-E to D-F sharp.

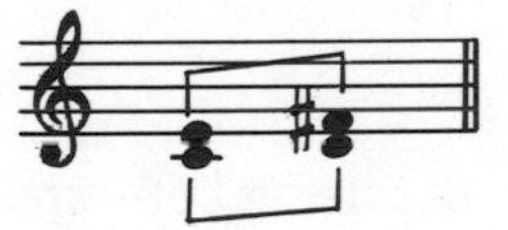

In the reverse direction, when playing from D-F sharp to C-E (from the 2nd and 4th fingers to the 1st and 3rd) special care must be taken to place the 3rd finger lower than might be expected.

In playing from B flat-D to C-E flat (a major third to a minor third):

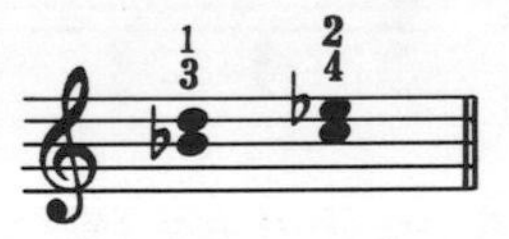

remember, from the discussion of spacial relationships of single notes, that a whole step between 3rd and 4th finger is a small distance and that a half step between the 1st and 2nd fingers is not especially close.

Playing from C-E flat to D-F (a minor third to a minor third):

a special problem is created because the 1st finger is in half position, so the 4th finger must be played forward, but at the same time don't allow this distance to influence the second finger by pulling it sharp—be sure it is placed back a little.

Playing from a minor third to a major third, such as C-E flat to D flat-F:

place the 4th finger close to the 3rd, as a half step between these fingers is a small distance; and a whole step between 1st and 2nd finger is a large distance.

When shifting the same fingers from a minor third to a major third, as A-C to B flat-D (with either 1st and 3rd, or 2nd and 4th):

the bottom finger, either 1st or 2nd, moves a large distance—two whole tones—while the top finger, either 3rd or 4th moves a small distance—one and a half tones. In the reverse situation, moving from a major third to a minor third, as from G-B to A-C:

the bottom finger moves a small distance while the top finger moves large.

Shifts such as from B flat-D to D-F with the same fingers:

on the same string involves moving from an interval of—speaking in terms of parallel distances—one and a half tones to two tones so care must be taken that the 1st finger is low and the 3rd is high. In the reverse situation, going from an interval such as C-E flat to E flat-G:

the 4th (or 3rd) finger must be low and the 2nd (or 1st) must be high.

When playing the same interval with different fingers (as in changing position) such as D-F sharp:

the shift is made with the hand, wrist firm, so aim for a small distance between the fingers.

In the high positions when a half step occurs between the 3rd and 4th fingers, for example C sharp-E to D-F sharp:

the 4th finger should almost replace the 3rd as the distance is so small; the finger should be placed on the tip so that there is very little flesh on the string. Play the 2nd finger high and move the 3rd finger out of the way to make room for the 4th.

3

A major seventh is played as the reverse of a minor third, as in A-G sharp and C sharp-E.

The distance between the fingers in the major seventh must be felt larger than the third because in this hand position the webbing between the fingers stretches; so the visual space for a major seventh must be extremely large. The space for a minor seventh is larger than that of a major third for the same reasons.

4

Sixths If you play on the D string from E to F sharp with the 1st and 2nd finger it is a large distance, as it is a whole step.

This represents the parallel distance of a major sixth, from E to C sharp, but this distance is even larger because the web between the 1st and 2nd finger stretches as you cross to the next string.

When playing a series of ascending sixths:

the finger that moves parallel across the strings (that which is common to both sixths) should be placed back a little on the lower string and the new finger placed higher. In the example above in going from E-C sharp to F sharp-D sharp, the placement of the 3rd finger high (which is as it should be) will have a tendency to pull the 2nd finger forward, for this reason the lower finger must be placed back. In general when playing passages such as this don't raise the fingers high, the motion should be sideways across the strings.

5

As in the relationship between thirds and sevenths, the fourth is just the reverse of the sixth. It should be felt slightly smaller than the corresponding sixth because the webbing between the fingers becomes more narrow.

6

Octaves Generally the 1st finger is much stronger than the 4th so when playing octaves if any vertical pressure is used the 1st finger will tend to play sharper than the 4th. Very little pressure must be used, and to compensate the shifts must be fast and stiff, made with a forearm motion. To set the hand in the octave position the feeling must be very comfortable and normal, not at all stretched because the space between the 1st and 4th finger is really a perfect fourth opened up slightly to account for playing across two strings.

Even though the 4th finger is weak it must lead the hand in shifting; it should be kept stiff to resist the motion of the 1st finger. The 4th finger stays fixed in relation to the rest of the hand, while the first finger aims and adjusts to create proper intonation. As would be expected, the higher the position the smaller is the distance between octaves. After the fifth position, even though the distances are small, push with the first finger to compensate for the thumb being locked in the neck; on the way back be sure the motion of the hand resists the tendency of the thumb to pull the hand back too far.

The basic concept of whole steps being large and half steps small holds true with octaves. In playing chromatic scales with octaves not every half step is equal. The natural tendency is to think of a half step as being small, and after a whole step it certainly is, but in a series of half steps they cannot all be played with the same spacial concepts. The general rule is: ascending naturals and sharps are large half steps, flats are small; descending naturals and flats are large, sharps are small. In the following example, in which just the lower note of the octave is written, a mark ⊔ indicates a large distance and a mark ✓ indicates a small space.

When playing dramatic melodies in octaves, minimize the sound on the top string; create the intensity of the sound on the lower note, as for example in the Sibelius concerto or Chausson Poeme. This will keep the passage from becoming strident.

To create the most comfortable position for the left hand in playing fingered octaves turn the left elbow in, close to the body and play with the side of the 3rd finger, rather than with the fleshy pad. Because the 3rd finger is stretched abnormally adjustments must be made in shifting—when ascending push forward with the finger, and descending always take care that 1 and 3 remain an abnormally large distance.

In playing scales and fast virtuoso passages the intonation with the 1st finger must be impeccable, then add the top note. In general aim for the lower note and hardly touch the top, playing both notes well only at the end of a run. In playing scales place the hand in a very "forward" position so that the 3rd and 4th fingers will not be so abnormally out of place.

7

Tenths To make the stretch of the tenth as comfortable as possible place the hand in a forward position and set the 4th finger on the upper note of the tenth, then extend back with the index finger for the lower note. Ascending the 4th finger which remains in a fixed, stiff position with the hand "leads" the shift while the first finger "guides" the intonation. Descending, the first finger both "leads the shift and "guides" the intonation. There should be no vertical pressure in the fingers. In the higher positions the 1st finger must move forward with greater effort to offset the backward pull of the thumb.

When playing scales in tenths the distances for each successive tenth must be thought out because each one involves two separate spaces (with the 1st and 4th finger). Following is the C major scale in tenths with a description where necessary of the spacial relationships both ascending and descending. Remember that all stretches are created from the top finger to the bottom.

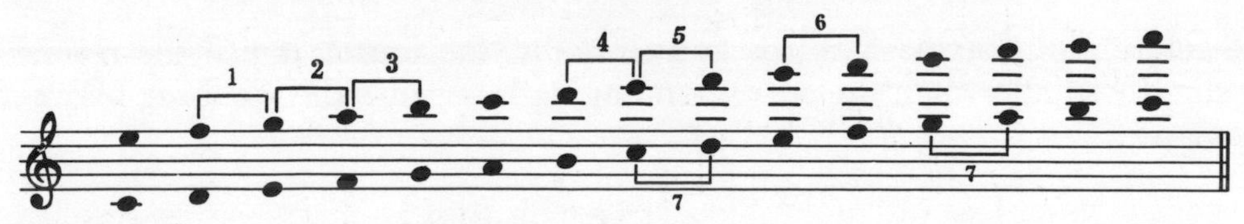

1. D-F to E-G: the 3rd finger on F is in the third position so place the fourth finger on G and just extend the 1st finger back to E for the next tenth.
2. E-G to F-A: Move the 4th finger a large distance to cover the whole step, but the 1st finger shift must be very small so that it is not carried along with the 4th finger motion.
3. F-A to G-B: When the distance for both fingers is equal—a whole step for each finger—the 4th finger motion must be a little more to compensate for its weakness.

4. B-D to C-E: Here, again, because the 4th finger must move a large distance the 1st finger moves only slightly.
5. C-E to D-F: The first finger moves a large distance, while the 4th moves small.
6. E-G to F-A: The first finger moves a half step which is small while the 4th finger moves a whole step which is large.
7. In both cases of descending tenths the 1st finger moves a whole step while the 4th finger moves only a half. The motion of the 1st finger will push the 4th back sufficiently to make it unnecessary to consciously move the 4th finger at all.

8

Fifths There are two principles to bear in mind concerning fifths: in general the finger must be placed across the two strings with more flesh on the upper string. My pupil, Dr. Vahe Djingheuzian, has suggested to play fifths by placing the finger as though to play harmonics (with the tip of the finger) on both strings, then push down to play fifths.

9

Consideration must be given to passages, as they often occur, consisting of several different types of double-stops—combining a variety of thirds, sixths, octaves and fourths. Keep in mind that the third finger should stabilize or center the hand. Place this well on the cushion with a firm, straight feeling in the wrist. This is most applicable in playing consecutive thirds or fingered octaves. After an "abnormal" chord (awkward in hand), return to "normalcy" immediately by centering again on the third finger. In these cases the problem must be solved by setting each double-stop independently. The first example of this is taken from Dont caprices Op.35 #21.

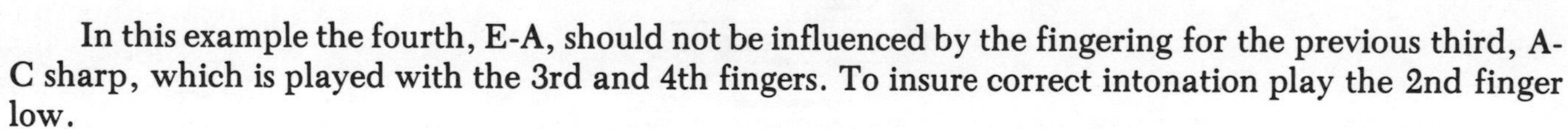

In this example the fourth, E-A, should not be influenced by the fingering for the previous third, A-C sharp, which is played with the 3rd and 4th fingers. To insure correct intonation play the 2nd finger low.

The following example is taken from Sevcik Op.1 Part IV exercise #2. The first measure is:

There are various combinations of double-stops which must be practiced separately to insure proper intonation before the measure can be played as a whole. The octaves form the framework for the whole line so they must be practiced separately as a scale:

then practice the sixths with the 3rd and 4th finger as a scale to determine which distances are large and small:

lastly, practice the spaces between the 1st and 3rd fingers on the A string to determine which intervals are one and a half tones and which are two:

when the whole example is played each of these must be considered alone and not influenced by what else is going on. Most important is to *aim* for the space, *then* listen.

10

Chords When using three fingers to play a chord as in this example from Dont Op.35 #1:

in the second chord aim for the middle note, in this case the 1st, and add the other two notes with the 3rd and 4th fingers. Another example of a three-note chord from the same exercise is:

In this chord first set the 2nd finger which is the middle note, then add the 3rd and 4th fingers. In measure 18 of this exercise is an example of four-note chords:

When using all four fingers for a chord aim for the 3rd note and place the others in relation to it. When playing diminished arpeggios with the 1st, 2nd, 3rd, and 4th fingers:

watch that the 2nd finger does not get sharp. The 2nd and 3rd fingers are connected in the hand so there will be a natural tendency for them to close the distance; a conscious effort must be made to see that the 2nd finger does not creep up.

Chapter 2
LEFT HAND TECHNIQUE AND DEVELOPMENT OF PRACTICE HABITS

INTRODUCTION

The purpose in examining the techniques of practicing is to enable the violinist, even the very advanced, to maximize the effects of a minimum amount of practice time through the development of constructive habits. In my many years of teaching and observing students and accomplished violinists I have discovered certain basic weaknesses to be common among all players. Useful practicing is based on overcoming these common natural weaknesses rather than relying on our strengths. Practice should enable us to overcome obstacles so that all our abilities are equally strong. This principle has been espoused by others such as my teacher Leopold Auer and other great artists. Most teachers and artists agree that the most effective material to use in overcoming problems is the careful study of scales, arpeggios, and doublestops; without fluent technique in executing these, playing the violin is impossible.

Being aware of what is happening and what is to come is of primary importance in practicing. Playing in a slow tempo enables the violinist to analyze critically what is happening and at the same time visualize intellectually what is to come. But within this framework of the slow tempo it is most important to use fast decisive actions with the muscles of the left hand. Practicing with fast muscles in a slow tempo enables the player to be in command of dictating the action with his mind and to develop speed in the muscles necessary for playing in fast tempos. Within this framework it is possible to make *every* note an individual and unique creation, each with its own initiative. Only when each note is conceived individually, not being affected by what came before or what is to follow, can a smooth attached line be created. This principle of detachment and attachment will be considered in much greater detail in the chapter on interpretation but should be considered on all levels of technical development. I believe that true technique and interpretation form an integrated whole and cannot be disjoined.

Learn to stay loose while practicing. Working with a relaxed feeling will lead to a more productive output and help reduce the natural tension and anxiety everyone feels while performing. To create a feeling of security and develop a deep full sound sink the bow into the strings. Play with a deep bow action without any intention of creating a refined sound at first. This approach will point up faults and weaknesses more clearly and lead to a greater feeling of security in future playing.

My system of practicing and developing technique is based on the premise that there are two areas into which our problems in playing fall—muscular and psychological. The first relates to the purely physical weaknesses of our hands and arms. The problems of left hand intonation and right hand bow control are dealt with separately; my concern here is the muscular interaction of finger motion with other fingers, the hand, and the arm. Examples of these obstacles are shown along with specific recommendations of exercises to practice so as to develop the muscles necessary to overcome those obstacles. The second area of concern—psychology—involves our limited ability to control our anxieties about playing to the point where the music becomes impaired or distorted by our frustrations.

DEVELOPING MUSCLES OF THE LEFT HAND

There is a basic paradox inherent in using the hands to play a stringed instrument: The right, or bow, hand moves with a horizontal motion while the fingers of the left hand move vertically. The bow motion is often required to be smooth and connected with a flowing feeling and must create a sense of space; in other words to paint pictures with sound. In contrast the vertical action of the left hand must produce an articulative or speaking character. A unified whole can be created only through a co-existence of these two opposite elements, and this can happen only if there is a complete independence or detachment of function in both hands. This duality or separation of action will in turn produce a complete entity. Detaching the individual elements in playing will lead to an attached creation. If however the basic elements are attached or run together the end result will be unstructured and detached.

Before discussing particular problems it is most important that the player be aware of proper standing posture and playing position. Stand with the body weight towards the left side and the feet slightly separated. Then place the violin on the collar bone, but be sure that the shoulder is not raised to hold the instrument. It may be necessary to use a shoulder rest of some kind, as the players comfort must be considered. The violin should be held so that the head of the instrument is directly opposite the center of the player's face. Try to relax the diaphram while practicing as any tension will cause stiffness in the neck and both hands and arms. A tightened diaphram should be used only to aid in projecting interpretation, but never in technical passages where the aim should be to play loosely with freedom.

When the left hand is placed on the instrument it should form a straight continuous line with the forearm. The palm should not be placed against the neck nor bent outward away from the body. The first finger should be bent so that the action of the remaining fingers is easy and that they fall very naturally onto the pads. When the first and fourth fingers are placed on the same string an interval of a perfect fourth is formed—according to my principles of visual intonation a perfect fourth is a small distance so the hand should be placed with a forward feeling of being towards second position. This way the fourth finger can be placed most comfortably. The thumb can be placed opposite the first finger or a little more forward, but never any further back as this would put it too far away from the rest of the hand and create a cramp in the muscles of the palm. The height of the thumb, the point at which it comes into contact with the neck, is a matter of personal comfort, however it should never be so high that the neck rests below the first joint of the finger.

There are two sets of muscles which control the fingers of the left hand: those that raise—in the back of the hand and forearm, and those that lower. Lowering the fingers requires little effort because of the natural pull down on them; it is the raising muscles which require special development to counteract the downward pull and thus create an even articulation regardless of which finger is used or whether it is being raised or lowered. The development of muscle control should be done in a slow tempo but with fast exaggerated finger action, then when the tempo is increased the finger speed has been developed and the articulation is clear.

The best exercise to use in developing these muscles is Schradiek "School of Violin Technics" book I, especially #1. For example:

While playing the open A string concentrate on the first finger—think about lowering it and at the last possible moment lower it extremely fast to maintain an even tempo. Because the first finger is in a "corner" in relation to the rest of the hand and the neck of the instrument lowering and raising the finger presents an awkward situation. Repeat this process with the second, third, and fourth fingers. Concentrate more on raising the fingers because these are the muscles which must be developed the most: Also bear in mind that the fourth is the shortest and weakest of the fingers so there is a natural tendency to move away from playing it as soon as possible. This must be compensated for. This type of finger action is what will eventually develop into the ability to play lightning-fast passages with perfect precision and clarity.

While practicing this technique be sure not to raise the fingers above their normal height before lowering them. The motion of the right arm must continue horizontally in spite of the extreme vertical motion of the left hand fingers.

One of the most basic problems in an exercise of this type is to overcome the physical obstacle between the second and third fingers; as these two fingers are interdependent extra care must be taken when using them. When the second finger is down on C sharp, as in the previous example, and the third finger is lowered to play D, the natural tendency will be to lower the third finger too fast because it is already being pulled down by the second. To compensate for this be sure to hold the C sharp for its full value (what I call holding a note longer) and lower the third finger fast.

There are particular exercises which may be used to great advantage in developing the left hand muscles, and the approach used in practicing these should be applied to solving all problems with the left hand.

1) Schradiek Book I#2—You should practice a few lines of this exercise the same as #1. Also work on this in rhythms, such as: and . The finger action must be initiated energetically and the motion should be exaggerated.

2) When you have to play an interval of a third between two fingers, such as:

the finger that is skipped (the second or third) creates an obstacle to the lowering of the next finger. Hold the first note to its full value and raise the next finger high before lowering it fast so that the articulation remains clear.

3) Dont Op.35, #8—Play four notes to a bow and raise or lower the fingers quickly as in the Schradiek. This exercise should be played in the dotted note rhythms. While playing the higher thirds hold down the fingers for the lower notes, then play through again raising the fingers.

4) Kreutzer Caprice #9—Place the first finger on the bottom note and the fourth finger an octave higher and hold the octave down silently while playing the written notes at first evenly, then in rhythms.

5) Play thirds:

first practice as written, descending also, with the same finger action as the Schradiek, keeping the lower fingers down. Practice in dotted-note rhythms, then play the exercise raising the lower fingers.

6) Schradiek Book II #1—play in dotted-note rhythms as many lines as possible.

7) Paganini Caprice #6—Advanced players should practice this caprice slowly in dotted note rhythms.

8) Place the first finger on A on the G string; place the second finger on F sharp on the D string; place the third finger on D sharp on the A string; place the fourth finger on C on the E string.

While pressing the fingers into the fingerboard slide the hand up *slowly* as high as you can, then down again the same way. Because of the physical connection between the second and third fingers they will tend to slide closer to each other. Guard against this by paying special attention to and preserving the space between them.

In practicing the silent exercises be careful not to strain the fingers. If they get tired let your hand hang down at your side for a few moments. Be sure not overstretch your hand.

9) To develop strength in the third and fourth fingers:

Play alternating back and forth while holding down the first and second fingers.

10) Place the first finger on B on the A string and put the others on the string very close together. Slide the fourth finger, while pressing into the fingerboard, slowly up as far as it will go, then slide back the same way. When doing this with the third finger place the fourth on the E string stretched out away from the rest of the hand. Repeat this with the second and first fingers.

11) To develop the muscles in the third and fourth fingers especially, hold the fingerboard with all the fingers close together and the palm flat against the neck. Turn the elbow out away from the body and slide the fingers individually as in the previous exercise. Pay special attention to the slow returning motion.

12) To warm up the muscles of the left hand quickly, hold the fingerboard as in #11; press tightly and release. Repeat this several times and when some strain is felt hand your arm at your side and you may feel the blood circulating in the hand.

13) Practice the silent studies in the Carl Flesch *Urstudien*.

14) Hrimaly Scale Studies—In the Schirmer edition play the last exercise on page 20 (the last group of scales in IV). Practice the A major scale with the first and second fingers, the B flat scale with the second and third fingers, and the C scale with the third and fourth fingers, all in dotted note rhythms.

15) To develop the shifting muscles in the arm play on the G string an A major scale through one octave with just the first finger, B with the second, D flat with the third, and E flat with the fourth. Play each scale in broken thirds on the G string, for example: A, C sharp, B, D, C sharp, E, etc., all with the first finger. Then play the arpeggios of each scale on the G string with one finger.

PSYCHOLOGY OF PLAYING

A secure feeling in performance can best be achieved through proper practice technique and mental preparation. Because it is natural to be anxious about what is to come in a performance, the player must be consciously on guard against anticipating. I call this "going against our nature," in other words, fighting our natural tendencies and anxieties. This can best be developed through slow practicing. Once we feel secure knowing we have practiced and prepared properly we gain the freedom to perform and project our interpretation. Following are several principles which should be constantly in mind while practicing. The ultimate goal is to internalize these principles so that they become second nature in our playing.

1) Subdivision—Try not to think of too many notes at one time. Our minds can deal with smaller groups much more readily so we must subdivide passages. Runs should be broken into groups with the first note of each group serving as an anchor for the following notes. Only when a series of notes is practiced in this subdivided or detached manner can the run become an attached whole.

The first example is from "Poeme" by Chausson. Measure #151:

The first finger should be set well on both A's before continuing with the run.
The second example is from "Symphonie Espagnole" by Lalo, Measure #37:

The G's should be played securely. Generally this principle can be thought of as learning to walk, each step must be made carefully, one at a time, before going on to the next. When subdividing a run in this way each group of notes must be an entity in itself. If there are too many notes, the first of each group will be swallowed up and the rest of the notes will not sound clearly. Guard against the tendency to rush at the end of a run by starting in tempo; to maintain equilibrium in the last group of notes broaden out a little so as not to rush into the end of the run. This will compensate for our anxiety and result in even playing. In the following example from the first movement of the Tchaikowsky Concerto, measure 97, broaden out on the last four notes of the run so that you don't rush into the following triplet:

2) Open String—When playing the open string we tend to neglect it and pass over it too lightly; it is not seriously considered because it is so easy to play. To compensate and ensure evenness of rhythm the action of the next finger must be energetic. Hold the open string longer raise the next finger high and lower it fast. Generally when practicing take care not to be influenced by what came before. In this case the first finger must be set well without being influenced by the open string.

3) Fourth Finger—Because this is the weakest of all the fingers we naturally want to rush whatever note it is used for to get to a stronger more secure finger. To offset this tendency and ensure even rhythm hold the finger longer and raise it fast.

4) Repeated Notes—One of the most basic principles of my schooling is that second notes and second groups of notes must be given special consideration to ensure an equality of all notes. This is especially true when a note or group of notes is repeated. The repetition must be considered to be more important because we feel secure in that we have already played the note or group once and tend to relax or ease up on the repetition and so cause an inequality. Be constantly aware of creating when playing. Even though a note or group is repeated, each one must begin with fresh initiative because each note has a life of its own and with each note a new situation is created.

6) Fingers Before The Bow—There is always a tendency in détaché or spiccato passages for the bow motion to anticipate the left hand finger action. Be careful to set the fingers well for each note before moving the bow (I sometimes describe this as the bow politely waiting for the finger action of the left hand), especially when changing strings. Several exercises may be used to considerable advantage in developing these fingers before the bow technique:

a) Kreutzer caprice #8—practice slowly to discipline the thought processes, concentrate on setting the fingers well, then moving the bow. Two other principles must be considered in practicing this exercise; first, subdivide the passages into small groups of notes, and second, to think of the first group of notes as a question to which the second group is the answer which must be given special attention.

Begin by practicing very slowly with fast raising and lowering action and gradually increase the tempo.

b) Saint-Saens "Rondo Capriccioso"—Practice the coda the same way as Kreutzer #8, and set the first note of each group of six well to serve as a foundation for the following notes.

c) Paganini Caprice #5—After the arpeggios the 16ths should be played with a spiccato bowing, also the Moto Perpetuo. Remember to subdivide!

d) Bach—The last movement of the G minor sonata and the first movement of the E major partita.

e) Dont Op.35 #2—Pay particular attention in this etude to the question and answer pattern. Think of the last note in each group as the upbeat to the next group of notes, and when two notes are slurred hold the bottom note and lower the finger for the next note fast to ensure rhythmic equilibrium.

7) Shifting—As I have said before, since it is in our nature to anticipate we must act against this instinct and play without anxiety; this in turn will create a feeling of security in our playing and thus allow us the freedom to express our true feelings. There must be no anticipation in playing shifts. Play the note preceding the shift convincingly, hold it longer while concentrating on aiming for the next note, then move lightly and quickly on the same finger through the shift to the next note while continuing the bow motion, which is also light.

When there are a series of shifts to be made the first is of greatest importance. If it is made well with a secure feeling those that follow can also be executed with some security. But if the first shift is weak it will invariably have a negative influence on the rest. This is especially true in playing arpeggios. In descending shifts take extra care to hold the note before the shift to its full value and aim carefully for the next note; the bottom finger must move quickly and lightly while the finger for the next note comes down securely from above the string. Throughout every shift you must maintain the horizontal continuity of the bow motion.

As you shift to each higher position from the first the thumb should rotate under the neck as you ascend until it reaches the curve of the neck. Descending, however, it should move to its normal position once the hand is in third position. When playing slow or melodic passages the position of the thumb should be prepared in advance of the shift without disrupting the note being played. During the time it takes to shift which might vary according to the tempo of the music or the desire for effect—the bow should continue to move but with no vertical pressure. In creating a melodic phrase the pressure on the bow should lighten during the preceding note before a shift and continue horizontally during the shift.

Following is a list of exercises which will be useful in practicing the techniques of shifting:

a) Hrimaly Scales—#6, especially the last four lines, and #8.

b) Kreutzer—#11, play twelve notes to a bow.

c) Dont Op.35 #17.

d) Following is an exercise which I devised. All the shifting techniques mentioned should be thought of carefully while practicing:

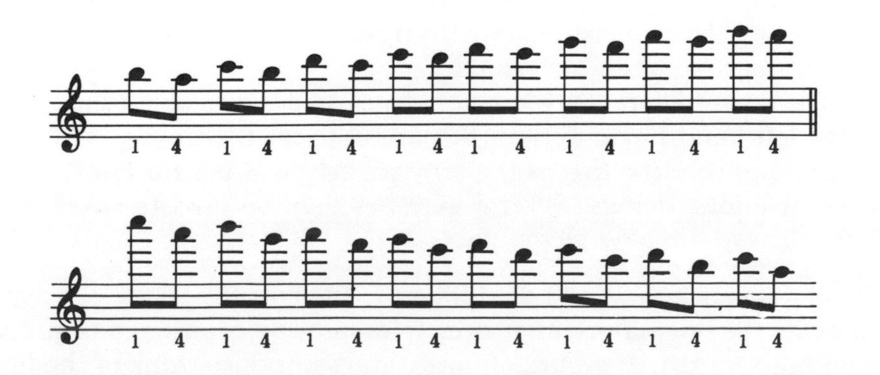

Repeat this exercise using the first and third, and the first and second fingers.

e) Dont Op.35 #15—The shifts in this étude are like gymnastic feats. Be sure the note preceding the shift is set well then aim and shoot for the high note. (I like to compare this exercise to an acrobat jumping from the floor to catch a trapeze which is swinging through the air.).

DEVELOPMENT OF VIBRATO

The following exercises are intended to develop those muscles in the left hand which we need to play a smooth even vibrato. There are two types of vibrato: arm and wrist. The finger is used only in conjunction with one of the two, each of which has its own particular character. The wrist vibrato creates a sweet singing tone, while the arm vibrato projects a more robust powerful sound. Theoretically the best type of vibrato is a combination of both motions, and every player should have command over both, but this is rarely the case. After developing the vibrato bear in mind that when playing with the wrist the initiating motion should be back, away from the body, while the arm vibrato should be forward. A "forward wrist" vibrato will create a wobbly uncontrolled sound.

1) To develop the muscles for the wrist motion hold the violin between your legs as if it were a cello. Place the thumb in the curve of the neck and the hand in a high position with the third finger down on the fingerboard. While keeping the wrist firm (not allowing it to move by itself) but not rigid roll the hand back and forth several times in each direction. The action should be initiated from the finger which moves the wrist especially in the backward motion. Repeat this motion in a continuous roll with all the fingers taking care that the palm does not touch the violin. Whenever placing a finger it should always be on the pad or fleshy part, never on the tip.

2) To develop some techniques on the violin it is necessary to train abnormally so that the normal presents no problems. Much the same as a runner training for a hundred-yard dash will practice running 500 yards. Hold the violin in position under the chin and the hand in first position with the third finger down. Using an action initiated from the finger (with the wrist held firm) roll the finger back then forward using a ♫. rhythmic pattern. Turn the whole hand as you move and the finger must be abnormally far forward so the knuckle is bent towards you. Each time you do this hold the forward position for several seconds. This is the most effective vibrato exercise and should be practiced diligently with all the fingers.

3) Reverse the whole process of #2. Using the dotted note rhythm first roll the finger abnormally far forward then back so that the flesh of the finger is almost flat on the finger-board.

4) To develop the proper wrist motion place the third finger on the fingerboard in first position. In a very slow rhythm roll the finger and gradually increase the speed. While this exercise in which the wrist initiates the action is not the most effective in the ultimate motion it should be practiced anyway.

5) Reverse #4. Play with a firm wrist and make the finger action move the wrist. Begin slowly and increase the speed. You might want to play with the bow for this exercise to see if the sound is smooth and even.

6) To develop looseness in the first joint of each finger place the finger on the fingerboard with the first knuckle bent outward. With an abrupt snap-like motion flatten the tip of the finger from the first joint only so that it is bent in; then move back the same way to the original position. Repeat this several times with each finger.

7) Place the finger on the flesh so that the knuckles are completely straight. While keeping the joints firm pull the finger to its normal rounded position with the action of the finger-tip, the hand and finger resisting this action.

8) Place the finger in a natural position on the string and bend it sideways to the left.

9) To develop an arm vibrato where the arm has complete freedom of motion place the head of the violin against a wall while holding it in normal position. Remove the thumb from the neck and make the arm roll each finger with a motion from the elbow. The action should create an exaggerated wide vibrato.

10) Place the hand in a very high position and vibrate on each finger, initiating the action from the forearm.

Following is a list of the works which I feel are most important to use in the development of technique:

Single Notes:

Sitt Book I—School of Velocity
Schradiek Book I—School of Violin Technique (Schirmer Edition)
Sevcik Op.I part 3—

Doublestops:

Hoffman—Beginners Doublestops Op.96
Sitt—Op. 41
Schradiek—Book II
Sevcik—Op. I Book 4. This is the best of the above.

Scales:

Hrimaly
Flesch

Etudes:

Kayser Books I-III
Mazas Books I-II
Kreutzer 42 Caprices—This is one of the most important technical works for violin study
Fiorello—Excerpts from the études
Rode—Etudes to be used in conjunction with Dont
Dont—Op.35 This is the most important book of etudes to study
Paganini Caprices—Flesch edition
Ernst Caprices

Chapter 3
RIGHT HAND TECHNIQUE AND DEVELOPMENT OF PRACTICE HABITS

INTRODUCTION

The function of the right hand in playing a stringed instrument might well be compared to that of a painter, and the bow to his brush. But without "speaking articulative fingers" in the left hand, the bow is ineffectual. Once the left hand is developed however, a great deal of subtlety and phrasing can be created with the bow.

Since the problems in the bow arm are mostly of muscular coordination the hand and arm must be developed through a series of exercises, much the same way as in the development of the left hand. The bow grip must be firm but yet comfortable and elastic in the palm of the hand. The thumb should be placed on the bow stick about ½" from the frog, but this may vary according to the player's comfort. The thumb should be opposite the second or between the second and third fingers; if it is too far forward, as opposite the first finger, too much tension is created in the muscles of the hand and the big muscle of the thumb. The thumb should be bent slightly outward , never in. When holding the bow the index finger should be able to curve nicely over the stick to give the hand a "secure," deep feeling. The tip of the fourth finger should be placed on the bow and must be slightly curved. No pressure should be exerted by the little finger except in crossing strings with a heavy spiccato. The fingers should be close but not pressing each other; if the first finger is separated too much a cramp could develop in the hand muscles.

In placing the bow on the string the weight of the arm should be centered in the wrist and first finger. To place the bow properly, bend the hand back and depress the wrist. As you rotate the wrist to place the bow on the string the whole line of the arm and hand will flatten out, and a horizontal line is created by drawing the bow evenly from the tip to the frog. For weighty playing, let the wrist "sink" more and feel the weight of the first and third fingers over the bow. This keeps the bow straight with the bridge and makes it possible to use a more compact bow space.

"Choking" up on the bow about ½" as I have suggested will physically shorten the bow, but psychologically it will become longer because the grip will give the player more control at the tip; thus the bow speed can be slower and increase the playing time in a single bow stroke. Holding the bow back at the frog, however, will create a greater feeling of insecurity at the tip and require a faster arm motion which in effect will shorten the bow.

When playing from the frog to the middle of the bow, the motion should be made with the whole arm from the shoulder. As the forearm opens a little the elbow should be bent at about a 90 degree angle; I call this the "border," from this point to the tip of the bow the movement in the arm should be a free motion with the forearm only. For the upbow, initiate with the forearm, then finish the stroke with the whole arm; take care not to raise the shoulder. In playing forte upbow you should be aware of the natural gravitational pull downward on the arm and compensate by moving the bow with a faster action, but with no accent.

Always be aware of creating a continuity in the bow motion, each note no matter how short must have enough bow space to allow the note to sound. To maintain an even sound in a slow single bow stroke it will be necessary to vary the speed of the motion in various parts of the bow. Whenever there is more vertical pressure on the string from the natural weight of the bow it must be compensated for with faster motion, as in the lower part where the motion should be fast with little pressure from the forearm. In the middle of the bow slow the motion a bit and gradually speed up as you approach the tip, adding weight to compensate for the lack of the natural bow weight. This ratio remains the same in the upbow motion.

1) To insure smooth changes at the frog a great amount of control is necessary. Practice tremolo exercise playing in the lower half of the bow. At the frog play four sixteenth-notes very quickly with a minimum amount of bow pressure and movement of the right hand, then play towards the middle of the bow and play four sixteenths again, return to the frog and repeat. Repeat this exercise using two 16ths and finally one. Now imagine only one tremolo still exists before the change. Keep the motion of the bow continuous with no change in the angle of the stick, and with a minimal flick of the index finger and wrist the down stroke will be accomplished with no anticipation or accent. The "imaginary" one tremolo "measures" the exact moment of the change at the frog. Be sure to keep the bow slightly away from the bridge in this exercise.

2) Kreutzer Etude #8—Practice a few lines in all parts of the bow, especially the lower half. Remember that the upbows require more energy and speed to compensate for the natural gravitational pull downward on the bow arm. Don't play too near the bridge and be sure all changes are made smoothly with no accent. When playing in the upper half use some pressure and move more vigorously with the forearm especially on the downbows to keep the motion free at the elbow. Keep the wrist motion to a minimum, particularly in the bow changes.

3) String crossings which are vertical movements in the arm should be made with the minimum motion needed to achieve the crossings with no accent or heaviness. When crossing the feeling in the arm movement should be more horizontal rather than vertical. The continuity of the horizontal bow line must be maintained through the vertical motion.

Practice the following patterns; begin slowly and gradually increase the tempo:

⊓ V ⊓ V	⊓ V ⊓ V
G D A E	E A D G
V ⊓ V ⊓	V ⊓ V ⊓

Think of this next pattern in groups of four notes. Be careful not to allow the action in the previous group of notes to influence what is to come in the next group. Use the whole arm maintaining a straight wrist line in the string crossings to maintain the same angle in the stick throughout.

⊓ V ⊓ V
A E A D
V ⊓ V ⊓

After you have practiced this exercise play these measures from the Bach E major Partita. First begin downbow, then upbow.

4) Practice this exercise to develop the hand muscles necessary for many of the following bowings. Hold the bow with the index finger and thumb. With an exaggerated motion move the bow in an upbow motion by bending the index finger sharply. In the downbow motion extend the index finger with an abrupt motion.
5) Sautille ("Uncontrolled Spiccato")—In using this bowing the rhythm and timing are controlled by the left hand action. The first note should begin on the string then the first upbow must be initiated firmly with the wrist to initiate the spiccato. Generally the bowing should be controlled by the wrist with little forearm motion. Keep the angle of the wrist and hand on the "upper" side; if the wrist motion allows the hand to drop too far, it is difficult to recover on the up motion. For a very crisp active sound the bow hair can be flat on the string utilizing the maximum natural resilience of the stick; for a softer sound hold the bow at an angle so that the hair is at 45 degrees with the string (this angle helps in controlling the bouncing action). With slower notes it will be necessary to play more towards the frog with a broader, more active forearm motion.

The bowing is built on four basic movements. Use Kretuzer Etude #2 in practicing these:

a) holding the wrist and fingers firm play each note four times with a stiff forearm motion. Repeat using three, and two notes.
b) Play each note twice as written above using only a motion in the wrist.
c) Use only the fingers playing each note twice, with an exaggerated motion in the knuckles.
d) Use only the index finger and thumb.

After these exercises have been practiced play the etude spiccato four times on each note, then three and two times on each note. Begin slowly and gradually increase the tempo. To keep the rhythm steady in the triplets give a slight accent on the second group of notes. When practicing this bowing it is important to bear in mind that the rhythm is dictated by the left hand. I call this principle "fingers before the bow". There is a natural tendency for the action of the bow to get ahead of, or anticipate, the action of the fingers of the left hand, which results in sloppy and imprecise playing. To compensate for this tendency and insure rhythmic stability be sure the fingers for the notes are set well before moving the bow. The left hand action must anticipate the motion of the bow, thus the phrase "fingers before the bow."
6) Controlled Spiccato—In contrast to uncontrolled spiccato this is played with a fast, sharp motion of the forearm beginning from above the strings. There are two elements that make up the bowing: fast space in the forearm motion, and stiff knuckles with little motion in the fingers. The upbow movement must be especially active to counteract the gravitional pull on the bow arm, and the fingers of the left hand must articulate each note clearly. The preliminary exercises to develop the muscles are:
a) play downbow and upbow with a stiff motion in the fingers, no wrist or arm motion is involved. The action of the fingers must be exaggerated.
b) to develop the hand coordination for controlled spiccato:
1) Downbows only: Begin from above the string and as you drop the bow onto the strings open the fingers with a stiff motion while you move the forearm quickly. In the rebound above the strings close the fingers slowly and keep them firm. This resistance will develop the muscles in the hand.
2) Repeat the previous exercise with an upbow motion: close the fingers quickly and hold them firm as you extend them for the next stroke.
3) For a rebound first only ⊓ -bows, then V -bows:drop the bow to the strings with a fast motion of the fingers and rebound quickly with the fingers to the same position above the strings to play another note.

Use Kreutzer #2 to study the bowing. It is very important to practice this exercise as written playing each note once, but you should also practice it playing each note twice in the same bow. With this bowing the downbow motion should be made stiffly with the whole arm, while the upbow is played more flexibly with the wrist and fingers. This can also be practiced in the same fashion with 3 and 4 notes.

7) Combination of Slurs and Controlled Spiccato:

This bowing is played by dropping the bow from above the string while moving the arm horizontally. In preliminary exercises hold the bow above the string and keep the hand arched abnormally high. As you drop the bow to the string don't move horizontally but collapse the arch so that the back of the hand is flat; with the weight of the wrist put pressure on the index finger. In the same continuous motion raise the bow off the string and assume the original position. This is the basic hand motion necessary for the slurred stroke. After this is practiced drop the bow from above the string and move horizontally with the arm, then rebound to the original position; repeat this exercise for the upbow motion. The controlled spiccato is as described in the preceding section.

To practice the bowing use Kreutzer #2 (Dont #13 for more advanced players) in the following combinations:

8) Martelé—To execute this bowing place the bow on the string at the tip and create vertical pressure with the fingers and wrist of the right hand. At the second of release of the pressure make a fast horizontal arm motion. The result will be a short note with a hard initial attack, with a pinched sound.

9) Staccato—This is strictly a virtuoso technique which some of the finest violinists in the world cannot execute effectively. Staccato must be conceived as a constant tremolo motion while proceeding to move up the bow very slowly.

Staccato can be achieved in two ways: with the whole arm initiating or with a wrist and index finger movement.

a) Play a tremolo at the tip with a stiff arm motion and move the bow up and down with a proportionally horizontal motion—this will create a staccato motion, catching or sounding only the upbows of the tremolo arm.
b) Practice the tremolo with the wrist and index finger and move the arm for ¾ the length of the bow. The tremolo must be continuous while the arm moves horizontally. On the downbow tilt the bow stick towards the bridge.
c) In the lower part of the bow where control becomes much more difficult bend the wrist upward more acutely while continuing with the wrist tremolo and horizontal arm motion.

The fingers of the left hand must anticipate the bow action. To develop this technique practice the bowing on the downward G major scale in the first position beginning on B (4th finger on E string) through two octaves. Be sure not to strain the arm and hand in practicing the stiff action; it is not used that much, not that important a technique, that you should damage muscles or tendons by straining them.

10) Hooked bowing—

First play at the tip with a firm motion in the whole arm. Begin with separate notes first upbow, then downbow; practice slurring two notes together both upbow and downbow. Repeat all these using mostly the fingers and the wrist. Practicing the slurred movement with the fingers and the wrist in the lower part of the bow will help develop the muscles for the staccato bowing.

11) Ricochet—Begin by playing on the string with no bouncing, keeping the hair flat on the strings. Play across two strings, then three strings, then four strings with the bow space very evenly distributed. When the E or G string is played twice be careful that the repeated note is played well.

With a loose wrist and no vertical pressure drop the bow from above the strings and move the arm. Each time that the G repeats make a slight jerk in the motion to keep the bow bouncing. Keep the hair flat on the strings, and keep the horizontal motion of the arm to a minimum; the motion of the arm is smooth and continuous, the bounce is a result of the ricochet from string to string.

Pay special attention to the A string in the upbow as there is a natural tendency to rush over this string in the upbow as there is a natural tendency to rush over this string, then to compensate and maintain an even rhythm play the D and G strings a little faster. Always play with no vertical pressure from the arm or wrist.

12) To play ricochet two notes to a bow, as in

begin by moving the bow detaché with the hair flat on the strings. Be sure to use the same amount of bow space for the upbows and downbows. Then move the arm with the same motion but drop the bow from above the strings; play with a very loose wrist and loose fingers so that the bow has freedom to bounce. Don't place any pressure on the bow with the wrist or fingers as this will stop the bouncing. You can practice the bowing on the following adapted excerpt from Kreutzer #38:

Repeat this through one more octave and in the same pattern descending.

In playing three notes ricochet as in:

bounce the bow as before, on three notes and "throw" the upbow with an exaggerated motion in the arm.

When playing four notes ricochet:

play with the hair flat on the strings and cut the last note as in the previous example. Drop the bow so that the hair is flat on the string and as soon as contact is made release all pressure on the index finger and move horizontally with the arm.

To play more notes in the ricochet stroke drop the bow from a higher distance to increase the number of bounces.

13) Rondo Capriccioso—measures 195-198, preliminary exercise: To execute this glissando smoothly begin on the E harmonic third finger and slide to the A. Mentally divide the slide into three beats; since the distances get larger as the note descends the finger must slide a proportionally larger distance as it gets lower. Once you can play the slide smoothly in one bow practice it with an uncontrolled spiccato bowing. Initiate the first note on the string. Practice then starting with second finger to the F sharp and finish with the first finger F natural. This is in four beats.

14) Wieniawski—Faust Fantasy: The glissando begins on the highest G sharp harmonic. Play upbow on the harmonic with the hair at a 45 degree angle, then turn the bow so that the hair will be flat on the string as you drop the bow (downbow) for the ricochet. Slide with the third finger down to G, then play the G, F sharp, F natural, E on the string. (The fingering should be 3,2,1,0 on these notes.)

DEDICATION

All my life I have had a dream of the consummate artist who would incorporate into his playing the many profiles of humanity, who seemed to embrace the whole universe in his vision. It is with great joy and gratitude that I dedicate the following thoughts on interpretation to my dear friend, Mstislav Rostropovitch, whose generosity of heart speaks for humanity and whose unique artistry has meant the realization of my dream.

Raphael Bronstein **New York, September 1976**

Chapter 4

INTERPRETATION

Every performance of a work is in its own way unique and individual; it reveals a facet of the composer through the eyes of the performing artist which makes us listen with new perspective, sometimes with wonder. We are moved by such experiences—moved to hear a phrase re-created with a fresh love and insight, and moved to great respect for the artist who has brought his own love into his effort to discover what is meaningful in a composer's creation. At times, the vision of the performer can reveal a dimension to a work which can surprise even the composer. I am thinking, for example, of Efrem Zimbalist's interpretation of the Glazunov Concerto. Zimbalist was a master of creating moods; his playing evoked such feelings of melancholy and nostalgia that when he played the opening bars of this concerto, Glazunov was struck with wonder and approval—Zimbalist had seen elements in the work which the composer was unaware of.

In his search to enlarge his vision of the music he plays and to realize his own individuality, the artist should carefully examine the direction in which this search will lead him. He can seek to perfect that which seems the most compatible to his nature—if lyrical by inclination, he will most easily see the lyric possibilities inherent in the work he is playing. If a romanticist, he will tend to bring out the romantic elements. He presents one profile. However, it is important for the performer to develop many facets—many faces—to embrace many styles and moods. By seeking to enlarge his flexibility of expression and of technique, he can discover an important truth about himself—that he has indeed altered, enlarged, his own "nature". He will see in greater depth and detail the "profile" of each composer, of each period. It is possible for a composer to express his entire view of "truth," of the reality of all things, through one object or aspect of reality—such as Sibelius expressed from his love of nature, or Debussy in his vision of water and sky. We accept their one "truth". The interpreter, however must embrace many visions, must recognize many "truths".

The sound which we hear creates movement and movement in turn adjusts sound. We hear sounds mentally and visualize the movements—this is choreography. Without these two elements, there can be no interpretation. The violinist as an interpretative artist works on this premise, holding intact his love, his "spiritual" vision of a work while realizing his love through "materialistic" means—through the organization of every movement of bow and fingers. Our first steps in the organization of sound are often faltering, as Walther's were in *Die Meistersinger*—the first expressions of his love, his inspiration, were clumsy, frustrating. The full expression of his love song came through his willingness to accept the discipline, what I call the "materialistic" means, of craft. We establish, envision, the character of a work—whether it is a song or a dance, a mood, a picture of nature, a story, or a love for the symmetry of sound itself. Then like a choreographer staging a drama, we adjust every movement of bow and fingers to project the character and mood we have envisioned. We know in advance of playing the speed, the weight, the space, the initiation and finishing of every stroke, the expressive "speaking" power of each finger. We work with paradoxically contradictory movements, the bow creating sounds horizontally, playing through the action of the left hand which is vertical. This choreographed action, this adjustment of sound, clarifies and enlarges our vision of the drama—as if the hand shapes the mind, becoming an instrument of vision and opening the door to the realization of our own love of a work, our interpretation.

We must also be able to choreograph the emotional content of sound through the control of our body muscles and our breathing. Think of an actor who is able to laugh or cry on command. We could learn much from the artistry of the mimist, Marcel Marceau, who through a movement of body and face is able to evoke a character or mood in a split second. To project a phrase which is very intense and connected and then immediately to change the character of the sound to one of introspection, pianissimo, involves the support and control of the muscles of the whole upper torso as well as those of the arms and hands. For intensity, support the sound from a strong diaphragm, the lungs full of air, which raises the whole upper torso and causes the muscles of the arms and hands to firm; the whole body feels expanded, tall and erect; the sound reflects this sense of expansion. This action becomes very complicated, however, because the constriction or tension must be focussed on the left arm and hand; the bow arm must play with a controlled feeling of weight, the shoulder muscles calm. To create tranquillity, the diaphragm must be relaxed, the breathing shallow, the muscles of both shoulders calm as are those of the arms and hands. These actions originate in the mind. We envision a cry in advance of playing, and our body reacts in its erratic breathing and in the contraction of the chest muscles. All of these bodily changes affect the character of sound. The fingers can create a role with a pressing action or one which is free-falling, playing with a vibrato created with a very strong wrist and arm for dramatic effect, or limpid, reflecting the calmness of muscles, the slow regularity of our breathing. There are important pre-requisites in the application of these techniques of conscious creation of emotion. First, they require a foundation of solid, healthy—ordinary—playing and cool objective work habits while a work is in the preparatory stages. Second, the advice which Diderot offered on acting: there is a part of the mind which must remain objective, apart, in the projection of a role—to allow an emotion to take over, to become emotionally self-conscious, will result in an inability to project this emotion to the audience.

As in the act of walking, the instrumentalist aims one foot after the other, creating each note, group of notes, each phrase "materialistically"—without anticipation—initiating and finishing each to the very end. Each step has its individual function and value in the collective whole. The artist is busy technically detaching or isolating each action, finishing one and initiating the next uninfluenced by the preceding action. In the G Minor Fugue of Bach, to play the subject the "same" on each entrance will not result in the "same." It will become mediocre, uninteresting. Play the subject, then start it again as if it were the first time that you have played it. This will create continuity. Spiritually a work remains attached, whole; the mind can see, can predict, what will happen next in the course of a work, can envision the total drama. But in execution, there can be no anticipation—each situation must be played to the very end, created with initiative and finished in order to preserve the total drama. Attachment is achieved through technical detachment.

Phantasy becomes reality when it is structured, given form and substance through a creative technique. If our phantasy, our imagination, remains in the realm of half-defined feelings or relies on spontaneous inspiration, it can become a detriment, even a threat to our existence as performers, destroying that which we wish to express. The greater the love, the imagination, the greater is the need for the artist to protect his vision through the discipline of primitive materialistic principles. The performer lives with the anxiety of being able to satisfy the demands of the aesthetic eye and ear. This "aesthetic eye" can be very cruel in that it demands absolute justice—is offended by clumsiness, by any sign of human weakness. It is the aesthetic eye which can cause a man to first react with a self-conscious laugh when he sees an old woman slip and fall, and then to rush to her rescue. We are all subject as human beings to both strengths and weaknesses, but the artist as a performer must become a prophet, above human frailty, in the eyes and ears of his audience.

A great part of the artist's struggle is in the elimination of weaknesses from his performance. He must be able to survive the judgement of the aesthetic ear by identifying technical and psychological problems and supplying the kind of physical actions and mental habits of preparation which will allow him to project his love and his humanity through his instrument. In the course of a long teaching career, I have observed that certain weaknesses seem to occur over and over again regardless of the talent or experience of the violinist: anticipatory playing where phrases are unfinished; inherent weaknesses of rhythmic control; inadequate attention to the contradictory movements of the left hand and bow arm, preserving the function of each in the total act of playing; unawareness of compensatory actions required to maintain equilibrium of sound and rhythm; unawareness of certain kinds of musical detail which the mind and ear rejects or passes over as inconsequential. The following primitive elements of playing, of approaching the ultimate goal of creative interpretive playing as we do the act of walking, aiming one foot after the other, are the foundation for a finished performance.

Second Notes

These are notes which occur on the weak part of beats; when there is a need for continuity of line or continuing sound, care must be taken to play these as strongly as those which occur on the naturally strong part of the beat. In some cases, second notes also assume the character of an up-beat. In the Allemande from the Bach Partita in D Minor, continuity of line is achieved when the second and fourth of each group of 16th-notes are equal in length and weight to the first and third. It is necessary to compensate for the inherent weakness of these second notes by holding them "longer" in the finger and bow. The second note of a two-note slur is inherently weak and the same care must be taken. The second note of a triplet should be played "longer" to maintain rhythmic equality and to achieve the feeling of "stretch" when occurring against a duple rhythm.

Second Beats

The same principle of second notes applies to weak beats. One and three being naturally strong, two and four must be played "better" in the left hand and bow arm. Think of this as a question-answer pattern where the answer is more emphatic than the question. A good example of this is in the Mozart D Major Concerto, first movement, measure 74.

In a passage such as this, the fingers articulate more actively on the weak beats while the bow continues with a symmetrical detaché uninfluenced by the action of the left hand. This passage is also a good example to illustrate the separateness of function which exists between bow and fingers. There is a tendency here for the bow to rush the fingers. The function of the fingers is to create actively the rhythm; the bow action feels "slower" in relation to the fingers—follows the action of the fingers.

Repeated Notes

There is a psychological reason why a repeated note must be played with more emphasis. We use initiative for the first, the second is taken for granted. See an example of this in the D Major Mozart Concerto, measures 57-59. The half-note G in M.59 is repeated, and unless played with renewed interest or new initiative, it will be insubstantial. In the cadenza of the Mendelssohn Concerto, the repeated notes in the ascending arpeggios must be played with new initiative. A beautiful feeling of equilibrium and classicism is achieved in this way. This is also true for the string-crossing passage which occurs later on in the cadenza. Besides the equilibrium of sound, it is also necessary to take special care of the repeated notes ocurring on the last note and first note of each bow stroke in order to maintain the riccochet action of the bow.

First Note from a Lower Finger

The lower finger (1-2, 2-3, 3-4) is held "longer," the next finger falling from higher than normal to take care of a tendency of the second note (higher finger) to fall too soon. Interpretation is dependent on the "speaking" power, the expressivity, of the left hand; never take for granted this basic principle of the lower finger to a higher. In the Mendelssohn Concerto, measure 76, this action creates a beautiful classical line in perfect rhythmic equilibrium as well as improving the "speaking" power of the passage. This is also true for the passage from the Brahms Concerto, measure 312, first movement. Hold the lower finger "longer" and then drop the higher finger fast.

In an ascending line (1-2-3-4), there is a muscular weakness in the rhythmic control between the second and third fingers: hold "longer" to the second, drop the third fast.

Open Strings

We do not respect open strings—it is as if they do not exist. An open string should be played "longer," the following finger falling rapidly and from abnormally high. This is especially necessary when the following note is on the first finger of the E string which is in a constricted corner (for example, the opening bar of the Prelude, Bach Partita in E Major).

Skipping Fingers

When skipping a finger (1-3, 2-4), bring the top finger down from higher, otherwise the finger in between creates a clumsiness.

The opening figure in the last movement of the Mendelssohn Concerto is one of the most concentrated examples for finger action and bow equilibrium:

Initiate the first note F sharp well, cross fast and light with the bow to the next note A, an open string, holding this "longer"; drop the first finger rapidly from abnormally high, and also drop the third rapidly from abnormally high to get rid of the clumsiness of the finger in between; hold 'longer" to the third before shooting for the harmonic (preceding note).

Preceding Note

The note before a shift I call a preceding note. Hold this "longer" in the finger, then shift light and fast on this same finger, lightening the pressure in the bow in the middle of preceding note. (Even if the note following the shift is strong dynamically, this principle is still the same—play strongly after the shift is accomplished.)

There is psychological anxiety involved in the action of a shift. By playing up to and holding the preceding note well, we take care of the tendency to shift too soon, an anticipatory action which not only blurs the passage, but does not allow the violinist to aim accurately for the following note.

FOURTH FINGER

We not only do not play the fourth finger well, but sub-consciously we want to get rid of it. Hold this finger "longer" and then raise faster. Aim with a slightly flattened finger so that the pad instead of the finger tip makes contact with the string, the hand supplying the weight or force behind it.

LEFT HAND ACTION

For most playing, raise the finger well, quite fast, the action originating from the palm of the hand, which is relaxed; let the finger drop freely of its own weight. There is every gradation of action through to a pressing one, depending on the interpretation. Leopold Auer used to liken the articulation of the left hand to that of an artist pianist, giving it an immense responsiblity and interpretative power. For fast passages, there must be no muscular constriction in the hand or the arm. Consciously relax the muscles of the diaphragm, which in turn relaxes the whole upper torso allowing the shoulders to drop. A good example of the pressing action is the Allemande from the Bach D Minor Partita. At the beginning, to achieve a very connected sound, "glue" it down with a pressing action, the palm and arm tight, supporting this also with a tightening of the diaphragm to add intensity to the sound.

In general, violinists tend to depend too much on the bow for interpretive effects. Think of each finger as an actor "speaking" its role, the bow constantly moving and "painting" the sound. This is a dual action, a conscious preserving of the individual function and creative power of each hand.

SUB-DIVISION

Our mind cannot grasp with clarity a large number of notes simultaneously. A passage must be subdivided, generally into two parts, but as often as is needed to have a clear mental picture of each group. Play the first part, then dismiss it and start again as from a first note. This of course is purely a mental process, and should not affect the sound or continuity of the passage in any way.

BEGINNING A FAST PASSAGE

A fast passage should be in tempo from the very first note, the end of the run not rushed. Our fear of a passage often causes us to start slowly, then to rush because we feel late. The last portion of the run must be more articulate and stubborn in tempo than the first.

VIBRATO

When playing straight-forward melodic passages, continue the vibrato through the note changes, and also the same speed from finger to finger. A delayed vibrato—or one that is faster, slower, intense, or non-vibrato, should be consciously used for certain interpretive effects. It is sometimes very effective to vibrate through half-steps shifts or even on longer downward shifts. For a warm expressive vibrato, the padded portion of the finger is needed; the extreme tip produces a much thinner vibrato because it is played on the bone-end.

BOW ARM-HORIZONTAL MOVEMENT

In the total act of playing, we must be aware of the contradictory movements of the bow and left hand action—the bow movement is horizontal, the finger action vertical—so that each fulfills its function. A good legato is produced when the bow is pulled through the action of the left hand and is uninfluenced by it.

SPATIAL DISTRIBUTION

For a stroke using the whole bow on one note, the second half of the note requires more space—let it breathe. (Very often we lose interest after initiating a stroke.) The purpose of this is, of course, to equalize the sound.

For intensity of sound, use a compact amount of bow; to spread the stroke diffuses the sound. Use more bow for pianissimo passages, the bow tilted at a 45 degree angle. For delicate "painting," remain near the tip of the bow. This is especially effective for a delicate shift: on the preceding note go to the tip pianissimo so that the shift is in "friendlier" territory. When shifting for a high note, also arrange the bowing so that the bow hand is pulling away during the action of the shift. When playing double-stops, keep most of the bow weight on the upper string. There is one notable exception—when playing octaves where the lower note should receive most of the weight to keep the sound from becoming strident.

BOW WEIGHT

To compensate for the natural weight of the bow from frog to tip, never press near the frog no matter how strongly you are playing; wait until you pass the place where the stick sinks easily into the hair. At the tip, it is necessary to play solidly and firmly. On a long stroke, the best place to save bow is in the middle. A pattern evolves then: bow speed is faster-slower-faster; apply weight at the tip, no applied weight at the frog.

OPTIMUM SOUND OF EACH STRING

For a clear sound on the E string, play close to the bridge, the A string quite close also. The full potential of the D and G strings is achieved farther away from the bridge. On a four-note chord, pull toward the bridge as the string crossing is accomplished.

FAST DÉTACHÉ

For détaché passages, use the bow from middle to tip so that the forearm takes over and the elbow remains free-moving. In order to keep the action free, it is often necessary to keep pulling out on the down-strokes so that the elbow does not bind.

GRAVITY

On a down-stroke, the natural force of gravity is working for you; an up-stroke must work against gravity so must be initiated with more energy. The speed of this up-stroke will seem faster and somewhat deeper to cover the same amount of space and equalize the sound.

SECURITY OF BORDERS

To achieve bow changes at the extreme tip and frog (the "borders") in flowing slurred passages, the last note and first note of each stroke should get equal bow speed, space, and weight with no accent during the change. A typical example of this principle can be found in the Chaconne of the Bach D Minor Partita, measure 59.

PSYCHOLOGICAL UP-BEATS

In a sustained melody where a feeling of intensity and of moving forward is needed, the mind supplies an up-beat before each note change and bow change. This gives a feeling of conducting your own performance. At bow changes, the psychological up-beat is the means by which the "borders can be secured" as described above. An example of this is in the passage from the Brahms Violin Concerto, first movement.

STRING CROSSINGS

A string crossing is comparable to a shift in the left hand: the preceding note is held "longer"—finish this note well—then move fast and light with no accent to the next string. For most crossings, especially in arpeggiated passages, use the whole arm, wrist firm, so that the equilibrium of the horizontal movement in the bow is not disturbed. In general, for repeated crossings in fortissimo, the wrist is firm, use the whole arm; in piano, move from the wrist in a small wave-like motion of the hand. (See the first movement of Brahms D Major Sonata.) For all string crossings, take care to concentrate on the horizontal movement of the bow, minimizing the vertical action of the crossing.

FIRST NOTES

Leopold Auer stressed the importance of playing first notes well (those on the first beats of measures). To amend Auer's statement, it is just as important to finish the note preceding well, giving to it the feeling of an up-beat, then playing the first note with initiative. This also supplies a better feeling of moving forward. In Dont Exercise No.2, every fourth note serves as an up-beat to the next group. See also the Prelude from the E Major Partita of Bach where the last two notes serve as an up-beat to the next sequence.

CLASSICISM

Classicism is the father of interpretive style. It is a basis on which we can build and modify to interpret the works of composers of every period. For me, classicism is like a Greek profile with its finely chiselled lines, perfect in equilibrium, each line contributing significantly to the total form. In musical terms, classicism suggests an unbreakable line, a phrase created with no anticipation, a feeling of rhythmic equilibrium in the balance between naturally strong beats and the weaker beats which must be played "better," the care taken in the spatial distribution of the bow. For example, we preserve the classical "profile" of the fugue in the G Minor Sonata of Bach by the care we take in matching the strength of the up-strokes to those of the naturally strong down-strokes and by creating the two 16th-notes with equal initiative. Many of the basic principles whcih I have described in the preceding sections have their origin as disciplines necessary in classical playing: second notes, second beats, repeated notes, spatial distribution, security of borders, first notes.

The classical "profile" of Mozart has always been very special for me. From listening to his operatic works, *Don Giovanni, Marriage of Figaro*, I began to realize what a strong correlation there was between these works and his instrumental compositions—and how this affected the technique of playing Mozart. It is as if each character of the drama, each face must be created separately, no two faces looking alike. Here is an elasticity of expression—of laughing and then of crying with no memory of having laughed—which demands the same elasticity of technique. Each face must be created with judicious use of bow speed and space, then stop, and create a new face. In application to an instrumental work, a phrase or a group of notes, or even one note, can be a face which must be initiated and finished before creating the next. We see then the work as a drama which must be technically detached in order to achieve the attachment of the whole. In his aria-like movements, we find the unbroken line, the bow creating a continuity through its uniform speed and smooth connections while the fingers "speak" expressively.

The classicism of Bach makes special demands on the player. He must give service, conform to the man Bach within the context of his age. It is as if we are permitted by Bach through the discipline of his music to express our own elation only after a personal sacrifice, a tempering of our own emotion. Bach spent a considerable part of his life giving service to the church. When we think of his work in terms of the unified architecture of a cathedral, of creating each note, each line, with the same care and finishing that the artisans of his time shaped and placed each stone, we can see that each note has its own individual function and identity in the collective whole. In some of his dance movements (I am thinking now of the E Major Partita), we see Bach also in an environment of 18th-century gracefulness and elegance. But mainly it is in works such as the Adagio from the G Minor Sonata where the strength of the chords support long melodic lines in perfect equilibrium, or the Chaconne with its expansive form and variety, where we are allowed to experience the dignity and expansiveness of the human spirit which Bach as a religious man envisioned.

ROMANTICISM

The romantic composers were aware of the need to contain their feelings and expression within preexisting classical forms. How does the performer accomplish this? Equilibrium takes on a slightly different "face" in the feeling of moving forward and holding back within phrases, and the kaleidoscopic emerging of moods such as those we find in the opening statement of the solo violin in the Tchaikowsky Concerto. In the first two notes, we create a mood of melancholy and a feeling of holding back in the slow action of the finger coming down to the B flat, an action which originates from the base of the finger, while the bow is glue-like in its movement. The next note, which is played with an expressive vibrato, changes the mood to one of expansive warmth. The phrase has a feeling of moving forward beginning on the high D (second measure), and a feeling of holding back at the 8th-note D one measure before the fermata. On this fermata note, count to four, each count proportionately slower, the vibrato less, the bow weight and bow speed less, to create the quiet mood on the final note on the count of five. By such a structuring of our romantic feelings, we protect ourselves from being "swallowed" by these feelings; rhythm takes on the dimension of "timing," allowing the phrase to breathe and yet maintaining a beautiful sense of balance. In the third measure of the Moderato assai, there is a beautiful example of romanticism contained in a classical framework. This is accomplished by creating the last two 16th-notes as if they were a "tear in the throat," holding "long" to the E, then playing the A in the following measure immediately in tempo.

In the Beethoven Concerto, romanticism must be contained within the framework of classical form. This is accomplished through the almost imperciptible "stretching" of, say, two notes to finish a phrase, the hesitation of a finger before continuing in tempo, thus leaving the rhythmic framework undisturbed. In the preparatory stages, practiced at a slow tempo, this action can be greatly exaggerated, enlarging the physical action and the mental picture of the timing of these two notes. Then, when played in tempo, the "memory" of this action still exists in the fingers and in the bow action without destroying the rhythmic framework. (See M.115-116 where there is an almost imperceptible stretch of the F sharp before playing the E in M.116.) Generally, the performer expresses his love for this concerto by creating the scale-like material Beethoven has used with great beauty and symmetry in the left hand, the bow creating an unbroken continuity of line. Sometimes these "scales" are highly expressive, moving forward or holding back in perfect equilibrium, sometimes introspective—and sometimes played with "no interpretation," an objective profile. In the second movement there is a great feeling of mysticism created by the warm expressiveness of a phrase which is answered in the next phrase introspectively, tranquilly. Mood is structured meticulously, as for example in the first three phrases: move forward on the first slurred group, play the second part of this phrase very evenly to achieve a relaxed feeling; in the next measure create the same feeling of moving forward, but much more subdued, and on the second half of the phrase hold back almost unnoticeably to create a greater feeling of tranquillity. The intensity of the third phrase is created by a glue-like action in the left hand, the shifts are also glue-like, deliberate. Every action of bow and left hand is structured, even to preparing in advance of playing the support of an intense sound by tightening the diaphragm muscles in the third phrase, whereas in the first two phrases, the diaphragm remains relaxed to create a more tranquil sound.

Sibelius is the last of the romantics. His concerto evokes pictures from nature, the serenity of water and woods, the grandeur of rocky heights. It is fragmental in character, full of kaleidoscopic yet obscure colors. The bow becomes a paint brush, creating the colors which one would see in the strange light of the northern winter sun, such as the passage in the second movement, measures 21-23. The bow creates a continuity of line with a flautato stroke using the whole arm, the separation of notes almost imperceptible, the bow speed slowing up on the last two 16ths. The second statement is quieter and more blurred in the finger action. On the third statement, hesitate slightly on the last two notes of M.22 playing these with a great melancholy and depth, creating the sound with support from the diaphragm.

When playing the music of Debussy, I see as well as the impressionist the impeccable elements of classicism. The violinist is sometimes a painter and sometimes must play with the classical clarity we associate with Mozart. In Webern, there is the beautiful fragmentation of material which is impeccable in the delicate equilibrium of each—a distillation of expression and material which is extraordinary.

We do not have to reject what we know of previous periods and traditions in order to play the music of this century—with the possible exception of those composers who are searching for completely new sounds. But we do have to expand our flexibility to include the wide leaps, the minute fragmentation, and extreme changes of mood in many avant-garde works. Composers are still involved in creating equilibrium of form, in the adjustment of sound in time and space. They only see a "face" differently, adjusting the "features" accordingly.

I have spoken of the classical "profile". There is also the profile of the interpretive artist. The 19th-century musician created his image by cultivating a mystique of the great stylistic individualist—his personal "profile" often superceding that of the music he played. This mystique is no longer valid. The present-day artist must be able to embrace many profiles, many styles. He must seek to develop and enlarge his emotional and technical flexibility to create the music of Mozart or Bach, of Brahms or Debussy. He must give service to the man in context of the age in which he lived and wrote.

Some of the principles for an artistic, finished performance offered in these pages are so primitive that it is easy to dismiss their validity as interpretive tools. But our artistic existence depends on the constant re-affirmation of simple truths. Interpretive concepts such as attachment through technical detachment, playing without anticipation, choreographing of bow and fingers, insure a performance which is admirable and correct musically, satisfying, as an interpretive performance. But there is a final reality. It is the heart, the love of the artist, which turns principles and concepts into truly meaningful, truly interpretive performances. And interpretation still remains a very personal thing. I am most interested in sharing with the violinist an approach which will ultimately give him the freedom to express his own love.

CHAPTER FIVE

TECHNICAL ANALYSES

In the editing of these works, I have chosen fingerings which utilize normal training, and comfortable bowings allowing for the maximum expression and creativity.

In the technical analyses I have indicated general mood and style, then focused on the violinist's attention on details which result in a "finished" performance such as how to achieve the timing and equilibrium of phrases of groups of notes, even of single notes. I describe the kind of left hand action and spacial use of the bow which will project the drama of a work—the finishing of each phrase, each note, and the initiation of the next.

Along with the muscular weaknesses which a violinist must overcome there is also the psychological anxiety of performance. One of the surest signs of immaturity in a performance to me is anticipatory playing, where the drama of a phrase is destroyed by a lack of attention in finishing this phrase to the very end before initiating the next with new energy, creating a complete change of character. The artist has a mental, spiritual picture of a work as a whole. But in order to project this drama intact to his listener, he must not allow this to influence his technical execution of it, which is a process of creating each fragment or character intact in itself. He creates through the means of detachment and attachment, a continuity of the complete drama.

Anticipatory playing is a result of psychological anxiety, of thinking too soon of the next phrase or the next note, of anxiety over a technical obstacle such as a shift or a bow crossing. A great part of the preparation of a work is in the elimination of these anxieties by creating a discipline of "stop and go" playing, of taking care that weaker beats and weaker portions of beats are played "better" so that they are not "swallowed." The objective here is to maintain an equality of rhythmic strength and projection; these should not be played more importantly. These inherently weak notes I speak of as "second notes": the second note of a two-note slur, the second note of a triplet, the second group which can be likened to the answer to the question stated by the first group, (the answer articulated "better" in the left hand), the second of repeated notes or of a second group of a repeated figure. In a shift it is the preceding note which protects the player from rushing into a shift. The note preceding a shift—and also a string crossing—should be played well, then the shift or crossing accomplished light and fast. (In a shift, lighten both finger and bow pressure during this action, then continue with a beautiful line afterwards. In a bow crossing, also lighten the bow action during the crossing and use the whole arm with the wrist firm to accomplish this.) A discipline of preceding notes provides the timing, giving the player the opportunity to aim for the next note.

The action of the left hand

The lowering action of a finger is generally fast, using the natural free-falling weight of the finger. The raising action is faster, initiated from the palm of the hand which is relaxed. In the control of rhythmic articulation, certain inherent weaknesses are still evident even in a well-developed hand. The independence of action between the second and third fingers is limited: ascending, the second finger must be held "long" (to its full value) before the third is lowered fast; descending, the third is held "long" and raised fast. The fourth finger has a tendency to raise too soon unless care is taken to hold it "long." There is also a tendency to ignore open strings; therefore in a combination such as 1-0-1, raise the first finger abnormally high to be sure that it does not return too soon. This occurs also in combinations such as 2-3-2, 3-2-3, 3-4-3, etc.—in each case it is the second note which should not be slighted. When a finger is skipped, in ascending prepare the second-note finger higher before lowering fast; in descending hold the note "long" and raise abnormally fast.

The action of the bow hand

In order to apply the natural weight of the hand over the bow, the arch, formed in the palm of a nicely rounded hand, must be flexible but strong. Anything which will stiffen this arch, such as an exaggerated spreading in the fingers will hinder the focusing of the natural weight of the hand and the cushioning effect of this resilient arch and wrist, thus adversely affecting the production of a full relaxed sound.

The bow has inherent strengths and weaknesses, so that the control of speed and weight must compensate for these. To produce an equal sound from frog to tip, the distribution of speed is faster-slower-faster; the weight of the stick must be lessened near the frog and increased near the tip, especially taking care here that the pressure is maintained through the bow change. To maintain a sustained line then, the bow stroke must "breathe" near the end of each stroke. This will also avoid accents during bow changes. The down-stroke is free-falling; the up-stroke must feel slightly faster and be played slightly deeper to equal the strength of the down because it is working against gravity. Bow crossings have been described in a preceding paragraph. In repetitive string crossings played forte, the principle of using the whole arm with the wrist firm is employed; in pianissimo playing, the wrist initiates the repetitive crossings.

Co-ordination of left hand and bow

Each hand has its own function to perform in playing, a vertical action in the fingers, horizontal in the bow. Leopold Auer equated the articulation and rhythmic precision of the left hand to that of a good pianist. The bow is dependent on a disciplined left hand in order to create spacially. The action of a finger must precede the action of the bow, the finger "speaking" the notes and creating the rhythm, the bow following or waiting for the fingers. The most common example of a failure to heed this principle is experienced when the fingers and bow become discoordinated in a fast detache passage—unless the fingers "lead," the bow will tend to rush the fingers.

For most playing, especially in fast passage work, the muscles of the abdomen and diaphragm must be completely relaxed. However, one of the most effective means of producing an intense sound in a sustained passage is by supporting the left hand action by a tightening and stretching of the diaphragm. This raises the whole upper torso, tightening the muscles of the left arm and hand to produce a very deliberate finger action and an intense vibrato. It is important however to take care that this does not affect a tightening in the bow arm action.

In practicing, develop in large pattern—in a slow tempo—the action which is needed for playing in a fast tempo. Raise the fingers high and fast, lowering with a natural free-falling weight. The bow arm is also choreographed in large pattern. For slow practice to be truly effective, the mind must dictate, must envision, the action and placement of fingers and bow as it will be at the ultimate tempo.

In every composition, regardless of period, the artistic player establishes the equilibrium of phrases, of mood and texture, which will bring out the uniqueness of the drama and poetry in a work. For me, it has been Mozart who has exerted the strongest influence in formulating style and discipline of playing which projects the drama inherent in the music. The discipline of creating through control of bow space and speed, of spacial "timing" in the fingers, of finishing notes and phrases without anticipation, of achieving a unification of the whole drama through a technic of detachment, all are derived most clearly from Mozart and are applicable in modified forms to all works from classical through modern. In the romantics such as Tchaikowsky and Brahms, there is the equilibrium of a phrase—of the feeling of moving forward and holding back; in the works of the French impressionists, the adapting of speed and space to "paint" the sound; in the moderns such as Webern, the extreme contrasts, the exquisite fragmentation and timing. Truly artistic violin playing is when the technical discipline and the musical of the player result in complete fusion.

In these editions, my purpose has been to provide bowings and fingerings which will allow the violinist the maximum of projection. In the analyses, I have chosen to emphasize certain technical obstacles and to analyze the means by which they can be controlled because they represent some of the weaknesses that are common to a majority of the talented young artists I have observed and taught, weaknesses in the finishing of phrases, the "swallowing" of notes, the maintenance of equilibrium, and the "speaking" power of technique. Out of the love an artist has for a work grows the necessity to eliminate any weaknesses that might mar its performance.

EDITORS NOTE:

The Bronstein Editions of the Beethoven, Brahms, Bruch and Conus Violin Concertos are available at your music store or from the publisher.

MENDELSSOHN CONCERTO IN E MINOR OPUS 64

INTRODUCTION

Mendelssohn was a Romantic composer whose sense of melodic and harmonic form and equilibrium was second only to Mozart's. Underlying the perfect proportions of the concerto is a tremendous sense of organization in which the great lyricism, even in the technical passages, is never lost. The picture created in "A Midsummer Night's Dream," which opens in a forest, can be paralleled by this work as the concerto opens with a picture of a garden. There is no mystery as to what the drama is, it begins immediately with its compact lyricism and optimistic freshness as if the garden were suddenly in full bloom.

FIRST MOVEMENT

MEASURE 2 The rhythm and tempo established by the orchestra in the opening must be continued through the solo entrance. This can be done simply by playing the 8th note evenly and in time; imagine the dotted quarter note as being subdivided into three 8th notes.

MEASURE 3-7 While the G—E must be played expressively, to maintain the rhythm hold the G to its full value, with no anticipation of the E before the shift. This E should have the feeling of leading to the E in M.4, which must be played more expressively. In shifting from G to F sharp in Ms. 4-5 hold the G for its full value so that there is no feeling of anxiety. This shift with the fourth finger is a small distance. In M.5 there is a skip of a finger between C and E; maintain a steady rhythm and hold the C long, raise the third finger high and lower it fast. Then, hold this E so that there is no feeling of rushing into the B of M.6. In M.7 be sure that the 8th notes are even; play the B with a deliberate feeling so that the second finger is not raised too soon. Throughout all of this, always be aware of the 8th note figures in the orchestra part.

MEASURE 16-17 In general, when a note is repeated, the second one should be played with more importance; play the second quarter note A more expressively. In shifting with the same finger, as in M.17, hold the F sharp long so that there is no feeling of anticipation.

MEASURE 36 The last triplet figure should be thought of as a question, and the first triplet of M.37 as the answer which should not be rushed. Play in the lower middle half of the bow.

⊓ Down Bow
V Up Bow

Concerto

Edited by
Raphael Bronstein

Violin

FELIX MENDELSSOHN-BARTHOLDY, Op. 64

58
sf
sf
sf
ff
66
C
71
p
mf
77
mf
IIa
82
pp
sf
87
sf
sf
92
IIa
p
cresc.
96
D
sf
p cresc.
f
101
p cresc.
f
105
dim.
109
p
cresc.

MEASURE 41-46 To insure rhythmic steadiness in these octaves place the left hand fingers well before moving the bow. There should be a slight space between each note. The bow stroke, which must not be martele begins small and gets larger. Play lightly with the fingers of the left hand and guide the intonation with the index finger. Play with a feeling of moving forward to the A sharp in M.42 and make a slight stop, then move again in tempo. Be aware that the space from A sharp to C sharp is a large distance and from E to G is small. In M.43 stop after the high B and prepare the finger for the lower note before playing it. The B—A sharp in Ms. 43-44 is played tenuto and on the A sharp move to the tip. When crossing strings use a small bow space using the whole arm and quick upbow strokes. On the downbows make the string crossings fast by dropping the elbow quickly so that the third note of the triplet is heard. The left hand should maintain the rhythmic initiative, otherwise there is a tendency for the bow to rush the fingers.

MEASURE 76 Watch that the second notes, the weak beats, 2 and 4, in each measure, are held to their full value and played expressively.

MEASURE 85 The bow stroke should be a compact detaché.

MEASURES 94-96 In this phrase when there are two notes slurred the first leans toward the second which must be held to its full value. Make the two separate notes even using a small bow space. In M.95 use a larger bow stroke and from M.96 on be sure the bow space is evenly distributed.

MEASURES 105-112 In playing these measures, be sure the second note in each group of three is played deliberately so that it is not rushed; hold the note long and raise the finger fast. The low D's are a completely different character than the upper notes and should be detached from them, played with no accent so the sound is even and beautiful.

MEASURE 113 Make a luftpause before playing the first F natural. This section from Ms. 113-120 can be thought of in two measure groups. The first measure is like a question and the second is the answer and must be played deliberately. Play the slur which connects each measure very lyrically.

MEASURE 121-122 In general when using a 2-3 finger combination there is a tendency to rush lowwering the third finger—as in this measure on A—B flat. To insure evenness of rhythm hold the note with the second finger long and lower the third finger fast. This is also true in M.122 on the F sharp—G. When shifting from B to D in M.122 slow the bow speed and lighten the pressure after playing the B and make a slight slide into the D.

MEASURE 124-130 Play expressively with the first finger on A sharp and D sharp. In Ms. 128-130 make a diminuendo. To create a tranquil effect, the bow should be almost flautato. Do not make a ritard.

MEASURE 173 Here, and in M.175, the triplets must be very even.

MEASURE 177-191 Underlying this section is a sweet lyricism which must be foremost in the artist's mind; this section must not be thought of as a mere technical excercise. Measures 181-183 must be practiced slowly to insure good intonation. In M.181 the C should be played "low;" that is, the distance from the third to the first finger should feel large, the first finger must be placed lower than expected. In M. 182 the B flat should be low; because by playing the D with the fourth finger the third finger will be pulled sharp, to counteract this tendency place the third finger for the C lower. The D—F natural must be felt as a small distance between the first and third fingers and in M.183, the last B flat should be played low. In M.191, play the triplets evenly and sing on the upbow. Do not hold the last 8th note.

112
III a
E
III
I
sf
116
sf
sf
dim.
120
sempre dim.
124
calando
p tranquillo
130
F
p
pp tran
140
guillo
III a
147
II a
p cresc.
f
153
G
sf
160
cresc.
II a
ritard
pp
167
a tempo
III
II
II a
f
cresc.
173
f
cresc.
p

H
I
K
cresc.
sf
p
f
ff
con forza
Tutti
IIa
IVa
IIIa

MEASURE 204-209 The string crossings in M.209 are made with a vertical motion of the whole arm by dropping the elbow for the crossing. In M.206 use a large bow space with a big arm motion. Ms.208-209 must be played with a deliberate action in the fingers of the left hand.

MEASURE 219-230 The character of M.219 should be very dramatic. In M.226 the mood changes in the middle of the measure to a more lyrical quality. The bow motion in M.228 must be piano when shifting from C to D: make a slight hesitation, slide with the left hand and move to the tip of the bow. In M. 230 begin the agitato on the third beat.

MEASURE 238-267 Enter as if the melody were a continuation of the orchestra line. To make the rhythm throughout this section steady with a continuous feeling play the first note of Ms.239, 241, 243 and 245 very firmly and be sure that the second and fourth notes in each group of 8th notes are not rushed. In M.243 when shifting with the first finger be sure the first notes, E sharp and A sharp, are not rushed. In Ms. 261-262 make a poco allargando; the last B of M.262 should not be rushed so as to create the tranquil mood in M.263. Make a slight hesitation before playing the long G sharp in M.265 and the first note of M.267 should be played firmly.

MEASURE 278 After the G sharp make a slight luftpause before going on to help in creating the character of the next phrase.

MEASURE 282-291 On the shift in the last two notes in M.282 play pianissimo and warmly. Broaden out and in M.289 slow up. In M.291 the first half is like a question, be sure the answer—the second half— is played more deliberately.

CADENZA

The opening of the cadenza is divided into three distinct sections of three measures each.

MEASURE 299-301 In Ms.299 and 300 play the first notes of the first and third triplets long. Then in M.301 hold the first note, play slowly on the second beat and in tempo on the third; throughout the phrase decrescendo to piano. When a note is repeated watch that it is articulated well the second time and be sure the note preceding each shift is not rushed. Play the final B in M.301 tenuto.

MEASURE 302-304 Move forward through Ms.302 and 303; on the last six notes of M.303 make an allargando going to the low A of M.304 and take time in shifting down. Play M.304 spacially the same as M.301 but crescendo, and play forte on the high A.

MEASURE 305-307 Play straightforwardly and evenly with no vibrato and be sure that the second groups—the answers—are played clearly. Play M.307 the same as M.301 with a decrescendo. On the last note—the trill—and all those trills to follow the note should be heard before beginning the trill. The rhythm must be insistent and stubborn.

MEASURE 310 Hold the chord long before playing the C sharp. Use a small bow space on the C sharp and in the shift to the E lighten the bow pressure. After the chord in M.318 play strongly and dramatically through the chord in M.322. On the C sharp of M.322 play with a sustained feeling in the bow, and become pianissimo. Hold the 8th note a little before playing the half note E.

219
L
226
p
agitato
231
cresc.
f
Tutti
236
p espress.
241
245
249
M
cresc.
253
f
f
258
IIa
I
262
N
dim.
II
III
p dim.
268
IIa
sempre piu
p

VIOLIN

al.
pp
pp
sempre
pp
Cadenza ad libitum
ff
sf
IVa
poco allargando
poco accellerando
f
Temp I.
cresc.
p
IIa
II
f
p
8
a tempo
Ia
accellerando
f
ritenuto
p
f
cresc.

MEASURE 323-331 Every note should sound clearly. When the upper note is repeated the second should be played more expressively. In M.325 hesitate a little on the second beat before playing the next G, then create a beautiful pianissimo with the bow. In M.326 the first C should be held a little but the rest of the measure played evenly. Play the first G of M.327 long, then through M.331 all the bottom notes should be clearly articulated. In M.330 move ahead in tempo and in M.331 make a poco allargando, and make a slight hesitation at the end of the measure before going on.

MEASURE 332 Begin on the string slowly, then in M.333 accelerate and begin the ricochet bowing until M.343 where the bow is once again on the string. A more detailed explanation of this ricochet bowing is in the Science of Violin Playing, the chapter on the bow arm.

MEASURE 373 Be careful of the bow distribution on the harmonic so that there is enough bow space for the G sharp.

MEASURE 414 Play dryly with no expression for two measures then in M.416 play with more emotion.

MEASURE 455 Make a clear stop after the first note before going on. The octaves must be played with a small vertical motion in the right arm. From D sharp play the octaves as doublestops; in playing this chromatic scale think of the sharp notes as being larger distances in shifting with the left hand.

MEASURE 478-479 Broaden the bow stroke on the D sharp—F sharp.

327
ff
330
poco a poco dim. e allarg.
poco a poco
accellerando
333
pp
336
339
342
1
cresc.
IVa
1
345
f
4
348
ff
legato
Tutti
ff
3
351
358
P
II
mf
365
sempre
piú tranguillo

371
dim.
pp
377
pp
pp
388
394
cresc.
fz
400
407
dim.
pp
a tempo I.
414
tranguillo
cresc.
419
f
423
f
cresc.
427
f
431
p

VIOLIN

435
cresc.
439
cresc.
S
443
IVa
447
III
cresc.
450
II III
453
ff
456
T
Tutti
Solo
ff
461
ff
468
Ia
più presto
ff
poco rit.
p
475
sempre piú presto
IVa
mf
482
cresc.

SECOND MOVEMENT

The artist's aim in this movement should be to create a sweetness and lyrical singing quality through a smooth bow motion. Within this lyrical quality the left hand action should be "gluelike". Each note must be such a beautiful creation that there should be a feeling of reluctance in leaving it; as if you were smelling the fragance of a beautiful flower and didn't want to put it aside.

MEASURE 9-14 The bow action must be spread out and special care must be taken to see that the bow changes are smooth with no accent; there should be an even distribution of horizontal movement. To execute the shift to the A in M.10 continue the bow motion and lighten the pressure but don't rush the shift. In M.11 play the last notes, D—A—F, evenly and not rushed. In M.14, as in M.10, the shift from C to E should be made by lightening the bow pressure and continuing the horizontal motion of the bow, with a slow shift in the left hand.

MEASURE 49 Play the last two notes, C—B, pianissimo and tenuto to lead into the next measure. In M.50 let the note sound before beginning the trill.

MEASURE 55 The drama in this phrase is created in the 32nd notes, but to bring out the melody a little emphasis should be placed on the 16th notes by playing tenuto on these notes. In M.58 play pianissimo on the last two 16th notes and make a slight hesitation before going on the M.59. The 16th note upbeats should be played especially beautifully and flautato in the bow; use a large amount of bow space on the first note. These notes must not be rushed and crescendo must be very dramatic, leading into M.61 which must be played with a full sound. In playing the octaves lean on the lower string without giving too much emphasis on the upper note.

MEASURE 65-72 Make a slight breath at the end of M.65, then in the beginning of M.66 create a new phrase. In this measure the third and fifth groups of 32nd notes should be played heavier; the same is true in M.67 on the first and third, and fifth and sixth groups. The last two notes of M.67 must be played quite deliberately. From M.68 the second notes of each group of 16th notes must be played deeper and more dramatically so that the notes are not rushed; this is also true in Ms.73 and 74.

MEASURE 76 The A should be played a little slower to suggest a connection to the G sharp in M.77; the G sharp and G natural should be brought out as the melody. In M.78 hold the last F natural until the two G's are sounded by the basses in the orchestra, then continue with the melody.

MEASURE 99 To create the necessary tranquillity in this phrase the B must not be rushed. Play this phrase with a smooth bow stroke and great expression in the left hand articulation.

MEASURE 106 Slow up to prepare for the end. In M.107 stop before the grace notes and play them deliberately. Make a slight stop after each C and play each one a little longer.

MEASURE 110 At first the playing should be simple and direct. In M.113 the G should be played longer then, after the F sharp, stop. The same is true in M.117 on the E—D sharp. Then make an accelerando to the A of M.119, and in M.122 after the B stop and create the next two notes as an echo.

VIOLIN

Presto

Grand Detaché

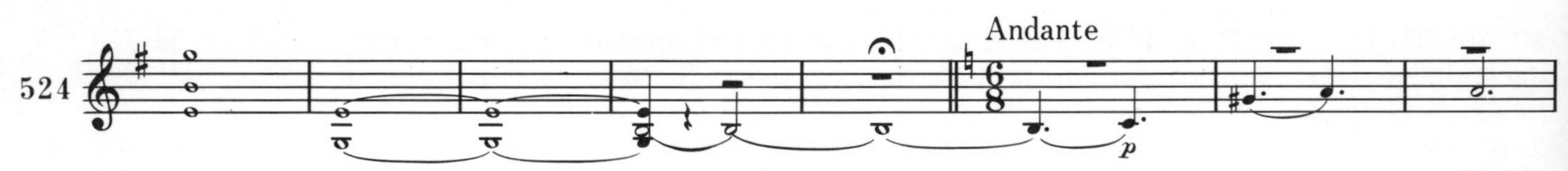

Andante

cresc.
dim.
B
IIa
Solo
Tutti
C
cresc.
D
dim.
cre - - - - - - - -scen-
- - -do
cresc.

VIOLIN

73
p
cresc.
76
E
dim.
sempre dim.
78
pp
84
90
96
F
101
sempre più p
105
Allegretto non troppo
110
mf espress.
cresc.
114
molto
cresc.
120
Allegro molto vivace
dim.
pp
ff
p scherzando

THIRD MOVEMENT

The character of this movement is reminiscent of the scherzo in A Midsummer Night's Dream. It contains the elegance and motion that Mendelssohn used in so many movements of this nature.

MEASURE 2 This measure presents an excellent example of how my schooling aids in overcoming muscular dificiencies and psychological weaknesses in violin playing. Set the bow on the string before playing the first F sharp. special care must be taken to see that each note is played in rhythm. Because there is a natural tendency to cut the playing of open strings short be sure to hold the open A string to its full value, raise the first finger abnormally high for the B and lower it fast. To compensate for holding the A and because the finger is in an awkward position this finger must be articulated well. Hold this note to its full value, then to compensate for skipping the second finger raise the third finger abnormally high and lower it fast to articulate the D sharp well. From the D sharp shift fast with a little slide; play the A with a fast stroke and cut the note quickly at the end.

MEASURE 9 It is imperative to establish a stable tempo in M.9 as it sets the tempo for the rest of the movement. Cut the first B short and articulate the 16th notes well by leaning on the first note with a positive bow action. To maintain rhythm in the left hand compensate for the skipped finger on the A sharp—C sharp by holding the A sharp long and lowering the finger for the C sharp fast. Use a vigorous upbow motion on the 8th notes, without making an accent, to compensate for the natural gravitational pull downward on the bow arm.

MEASURE 11-20 Play with a short bow space but accent each B a little to keep the pulsations steady. In M.20 play the grace notes fast and use a rapid upbow motion.

MEASURE 30 Watch that the first note of the last group of 16th notes is articulated well. In M.34 hold the note preceding each harmonic long and cut the harmonic short with a clipped bow stroke.

MEASURE 43-52 Use a small bow space and play with a whole arm motion with a firm wrist. In M.51 make the connection from the last A to the next G sharp obvious by playing them more deliberately; lean toward the lower note.

MEASURE 63-67 The 8th notes in M.63 must be played short and crisp. In M.66 after the last note, F sharp, stop to create a new more lyrical character in M.67.

MEASURE 79-90 Play quietly in M.79. In M.80 the B—E must be played pianissimo with a small bow space and very casual character, but in perfect rhythm. In the following 16th notes when a note is repeated watch that the second note is played more deliberately, as in the connections from Ms. 81—82, 83—84, 85—86, and 89—90.

MEASURE 107-117 The lyrical and expressive character here is created with a free flowing bow motion, but the tempo must not be rushed. In M.117 after the B stop to prepare the E sharp. Play the following 8th notes in rhythm.

MEASURE 149-167 To maintain rhythmic stability subdivide this run; on the D sharp make a very slight accent. Ms.166-167 are played the same as Ms.79-80.

MEASURE 176-187 Play these arpeggios on the string. In M.179 to catch all three strings on the upbow stroke pull the right elbow back a little so that the bow moves parallel to the bridge. In M.180 the last two notes are played slower. Each note in Ms.183-187 should be heard clearly before playing the trill.

MEASURE 197 Play the downbows very short and make a slide from E to C sharp.

MEASURE 230 On the upbows pull the right elbow back a little to keep the bow parallel with the bridge, and in M.232 the first note of the third beat, make a slight accent.

VIOLIN

cresc.
pp leggiero
sempre pp leggiero
G
H
cresc.

p leggiero
spiccato
Detaché
sf
cresc.
f
più f
I
brilliante
ff
Tutti
p
Solo I
II
sf
I a
cresc.
dim.
p semplice
K
pp leggiero
segue

84
87
90
detache
poco a poco cresc.
93
pizz. arco.
pizz. arco.
Tutti
96
Solo
dim.
99
102
105
L
espress.
109
Ia
cresc.
115
119

123
cresc.
127
f
p
leggiero
dim.
Ossia
pp
tranquillo
M
131
senza ritardare e leggiereo
135
138
141
144
cresc.
molto cresc.
147
sf
ff
N
Tutti
Solo
150
p
cresc.
Tutti
Solo
154
ff
p
cresc.
158
sf
p
cresc.
p
cresc.

163
semplice
IIIa
168
leggiero
segue
171
174
detache
cresc.
177
sempre più
180
poco allarg
Tutti
184
II
I
dim.
cresc.
193
196
IV
199
203

205
cresc.
207
f
fp
209
211
f
cresc.
213
IIa
sempre cresc.
215
piú f
217
ff
con forza e pesante
sf
sf
piú presto
R
222
sf
224
sf
ff
227
231
f
f

MOZART CONCERTO IN D MAJOR (K.218)

INTRODUCTION

More than any other composer, for me, Mozart has provided a basis for artistic disciplined playing. The clarity, the classicism, and most importantly his operatic genius has enabled me to identify and define most clearly what constitutes the elements of a truly artistic finished performance, and to apply and modify these principles to composers of every period.

There is a sculptured quality to Mozart's works which evokes the sense of symmetry which can be likened to a Greek statue—classicism in its most refined and chiselled form. We respond to his music in much the same way that we would respond visually to the clean lines and surface planes of a sculptured profile with its contrasts of light and shadow, evoking a feeling of sensousness or emotion which is tactile in nature. This reaction can be contrasted with, say, Beethoven whose music evokes a feeling of earthiness, as if it were possible to dig down into the depths of the human spirit. This suggests to the violinist one key to the playing of Mozart—of an architectural, spatial action in the bow which creates "contrasting planes" through a disciplined use of space and speed of stroke.

The first movement of this concerto is a fine example of Mozart's incorporation of operatic compositional techniques into an instrumental work. The unification or total drama of this movement is through a technique of detachment in order to achieve attachment: of creating a phrase, a group of notes, or even one note, then initiating the next uninfluenced by the action of the preceding group or phrases. Think of *Marriage of Figaro* or *Don Giovanni* in which each character creates his own drama or "face" (and no two faces look alike!), sometimes in solo, sometimes in ensemble, yet never losing his own individuality. We conceive spiritually and artistically the total unified drama; technically, materially, we achieve this by clarifying the contrasting faces, creating each separately.

The violinist creates through horizontal control of bow speed and space the "face" of one group of notes—sometimes a phrase, sometimes two or even one note can represent a face—finishing this, then initiates the next face uninfluenced by the preceding action. The fingers of the left hand create or "speak" as if each were an individual actor in the drama maintaining rhythmic justice.

The slow movement is essentially an aria, much more connected in its execution. The last movement has themes which are naively peasant-like.

Creating without anticipation, initiating and finishing well each phrase, each note, is of course the criterion for artistic playing of any composer of any period. But it is in Mozart where this discipline is most clearly defined and most exact, demanding a fusion of artistry and equilibrium of craft. Without a technical approach which includes a choreographing of the bow and left hand, we are jeopardizing the love that we have for a work; technique, when it incorporates this love and becomes creative technique, allows us that freedom and elasticity of expression which is so precious to the artist.

We do not have to reject what we know of previous periods and traditions in order to play the music of this century—with the possible exception of those composers who are searching for completely new sounds. But we do have to expand our flexibility to include the wide leaps, the minute fragmentation, and extreme changes of mood in many avant-garde works. Composers are still involved in creating equilibrium of form, in the adjustment of sound in time and space. They only see a "face" differently, adjusting the "features" accordingly.

I have spoken of the classical "profile." There is also the profile of the interpretive artist. The 19th-century musician created his image by cultivating a mystique of the great stylistic individualist—his personal "profile" often superceding that of the music he played. This mystique is no longer valid. The present-day artist must be able to develop and enlarge his emotional and technical flexibility to create the music of Mozart or Bach, of Brahms or Debussy. He must give service to the man in context of the age in which he lived and wrote.

CONCERTO No. 4
D DUR RÉ MAJEUR D MAJOR

Some of the principles for an artistic, finished performance offered in these pages are so primitive that it is easy to dismiss their validity as interpretive tools. But our artistic existence depends on the constant re-affirmation of simple truths. Interpretive concepts such as attachment through technical detachment, playing without anticipation, choreographing of bow and fingers, insure a performance which is admirable and correct musically, satisfying, as an interpretive performance. But there is a final reality. It is the heart, the love of the artist, which turns principles and concepts into truly meaningful, truly interpretive performances. And interpretaion still remains a very personal thing. I am most interested in sharing with the violinist an approach which will ultimately give him the freedom to express his own love.

ALLEGRO

M. 42-45 These opening measures are created as one "face" using a uniformly fast bow speed. The 8th-notes in M. 44 are played near the frog, slightly off the string, taking care that the up-strokes equal the down-strokes in speed and character of sound. Also take care that the second half of this measure is articulated "better" than the first half. In repeated figures it is often characteristic that the repetition loses in engergy unless it is consciously compensated for. On the final D of the phrase, M. 45, "conduct" the finishing of this note by "cutting" the stroke precisely on the second beat. To create the character of this phrase or "face" then is accomplished by knowing in advance of playing the initiation, the speed and weight, and the finishing of each stroke—play, then don't play.

M.45-49 To initiate the up-beat to M.46, place the bow in the lower middle, also preparing the fourth finger substantially. Raise this fourth finger well, fast and abnormally high, to ensure that the C sharp speaks and receives its full rhythmic value. This C sharp, because it is the second note of a slur and also on the weak part of a beat is often "swallowed" unless special care is taken. The bow speed for the 8th-notes in M.46 is somewhat slower than for the first phrase. At M.47, create a new face (a small sforzando) on the trill figure. This figure has nothing to do with the previous notes. The A sharp-B-A sharp is yet another face, lyrical in nature. Again in M.49, create a "sforzando face" on the trill figure.

M. 50-56 Finish the F sharp-G with a slight cut, then play the next G with an expressive left hand and larger bow space. In M.52, think of the first group of 16ths as a question, the second group an answer—the answer being more important than the question. This gives a feeling of moving forward yet maintaining a stubborn tempo—one of those seemingly contradictory paradoxes which the musician must recognize. At M.54, stop after the first 8th-note, then play the second note with a larger bow space and faster bow speed. This enables the player to recover his equilibrium, to get on the right track for the rest of the measure.

M. 57-61 The up-beat 8th-notes lean toward the E, the first beat of the next measure. In M. 59, the dotted quarter-note G is played slightly deeper and slightly detached from the first G. In M. 61, the F sharp (on the second beat) is not so detached from the first F sharp.

M. 64-65 Starting on the third beat, each bow stroke is fast and slightly separated. The up-bows must be especially active since they are moving against gravity.

M. 66-74 Use a fast energetic arm stroke for the first two beats of measures 66 and 67. At M. 68, create another "face" less energetic on the 8th-notes, except for the last 8th in the measure which is one face by itself. Stop before this 8th and create it separately. At M. 72 sing generously. At M. 74, again think of each group of 16th-notes as question-answer, being careful not to rush the answer. Bear in mind that the bow action remains the same, the sound unaffected in any way; question-answer applies to the left hand only, the fingers taking the initiative rhythmically, playing deliberately and never allowing the bow to rush the action of the fingers.

M. 79-82 Initiate the trill on the lower note, G. In M. 80, the two 16ths are one face, the quarter-note created individually, beautifully, with a horizontal almost flautato stroke. In M. 82, separately bowed 16ths should never compete in bow space with the slurred; take care to use a small amount of bow for them.

54
PT.
(espr.)
60
63
67
71
(espress.)
74
76
(legg.)
78
82
85
(espr.)
90
94
pt.
mp

M. 87-97 Take care to raise the third finger higher than normal so as not to return too soon after the D sharp (this note has a tendency to be swallowed). The G sharp-B-D at M. 88 and also M. 92 is one face, dramatic in character. Use a small bow space on the 16ths. At M. 93, cut the second notes of each slur short. At M. 95 use a smaller bow space for the last 16th note of this measure, stopping after the high D to create the three E's very energetically and short. Then create the A with a fast long flautato stroke. (For me, this is the humor of Leporello in Don Giovanni.)

M. 99-106 Initiate each trill with a slight pinch with the bow, then cut the note following. At M. 103, the finger action is like iron, the bow action "silky." Hold "long," to its full value, the first note of each, cut the second; raise and lower the fingers very fast after the first notes. At M. 105, play the second group of 8ths on the string and more strongly than the first group. In M. 106, initiate the second A more strongly than the first; cut the second note of each slur.

M. 115-127 This section is lyrical in character, becoming more dramatic on the second G of M. 117. Play M. 118 more deliberately until the last two 16th-notes which should prepare for the lyricism of the following phrase. At M. 124, cut the second note of each slur short. At M. 125, lower the finger slowly, deliberately to the F sharp. At M. 126, use a small bow space for the single 16ths (no competition with the slurred notes). At M. 127, play very objectively using a very small bow like the small tick of a watch.

M. 134-145 The first note is played elegantly and beautifully, then continue with no particular initiative until the last four 16ths where one must pay attention. This has a double purpose: firstly, the first 16ths take no especial effort of the mind to remember so that this sub-division provides for a clarification, of "aiming," for the second half of each group of 16ths; secondly, the last group provides a feeling of an up-beat into the next measure, and should be played "better." Raise fingers higher than normal in this passage (e.g. the third finger G to first finger B) to get rid of the feeling of clumsiness caused by the finger in between when notes are skipped. The first note of M. 135 is played flautato, beautifully. At measures 140 and 141, these first notes become more dramatic. The trills at M. 142 are initiated with a slight pinch in the bow and the second notes are cut. The long A at M. 143 is dramatic in character. The A's an octave lower are played flautato. Then stop and create the lowest A with a slower-faster-slower bow speed. Stop, then initiate the next phrase as in M. 57.

M. 155-156 The slurred group is played near the tip with very little bow, then cut distinctly creating the staccato note with a separate face. The second part of M. 156 should be played very deliberately and dramatically.

Cadenza-Joachim

This begins tranquilly, the second group of slurred 8ths more deliberate than the first. The first two beats of M. 214 are still tranquil with a poco accelerando on the last two beats, then poco allargando approaching the fermata. Stop after the first phrase, M. 215-216, and play the second phrase as if an answer to the first. In M. 217, there is a feeling of moving forward through to M. 219. Play the chords deliberately, then stop before initiating the 16ths. At M. 222 there is a feeling of moving forward as in the previous passage.

At M. 225, each group of two 16ths and 8th are initiated with a pinch near the tip of the bow. At M. 228 start to enlarge the bow space and slow down approaching the fermata. The 16th-note run in M. 230 is fiery in character, the following chords majestic. The run is again fiery.

At M. 235, play the double-stop 8th-notes broadly, bringing out the top notes. On the last two groups of 16ths, the third and fourth notes in these should be played more substantially. At M. 239, play very rhythmically with a very close bow action between the short and long chords (16th to quarter).

At M. 243, play near the tip, using the whole arm, firm wrist, for the string crossings. Keep the bow space small and the amount of verticle arm motion to accomplish the crossings minimal. At M. 249 and 250, do not rush the answers on the second and fourth beats. At M. 255, hold the double-stop long at the second fermata, then stop before playing the next double-stop16th which leads into the orchestra tutti.

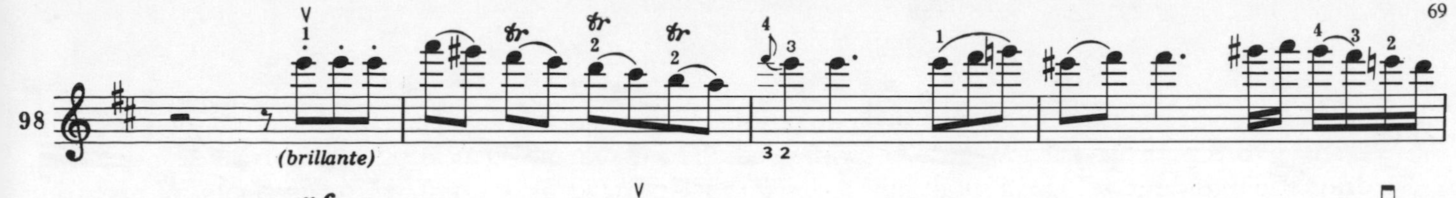
98
(brillante)

102
mf
(p)

105
cresc.
Tutti
f

110

113
Solo
p
(p)

117
(espr.)

120
II
I

125
(f)
(p)

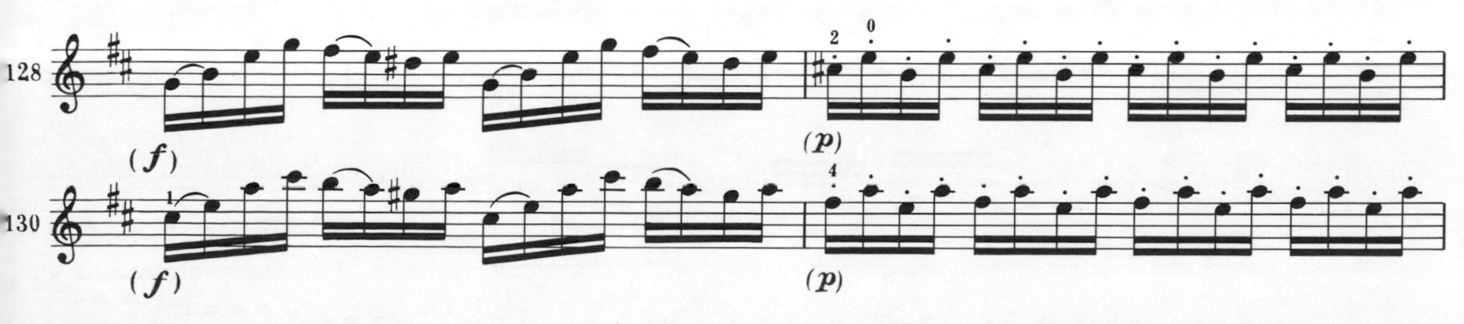
128
(f)
(p)
130
(f)
(p)

132
(f)
(p)
134
p
(mf)
p
mf
mp
mf

137
mp
mf
f
140
mp
145
(p ma con suono)
I
149
f
152
PT. p
156
(mf)
p
160
tr
163
mf)
166
(legg.)
168
f)
171
(p)
174
II

(espr.)
mf (brillante)
(p)
cresc.
Tutti
*) Cadenza di Joseph Joachim
Solo
poco accel
dim.
delicatamente
poco allarg.
espr.
calando
in tempo

224
pt.
p scherzando
227
cresc.
poco
allarg.
230
brillante
ten.
f
allarg.
mp
233
p
cresc.
236
cresc.
poco
a
poco
ed
238
allarg.
in tempo
f
242
pt.
p
brillante
245
p
248
crescendo
251
con fuoco
254
Tutti
f
259
p
f

ANDANTE CANTABILE

M. 11-21 Maintain a tranquillity and steadiness of bow speed and weight throughout, especially taking care that the up-strokes in M. 11 and 13 do not disturb the continuity of sound with any increase in speed in an attempt to recover bow space. There should be no bow accent audible in changes of stroke. The vibrato should reflect the same tranquillity and consistency from finger to finger, except for the sfp's in M. 12 and 14 which are brought out with a greater intensity of the left hand.

In M. 17, maintain the even flow, avoiding a portamento. At M. 18, finish the trill figure, then create a new face, playing the 8th-notes deliberately in the fingers. In M. 20, hesitate in the finger on the D sharp before resolving to the E. At M. 21 the left hand is expressive, the finger raising lazily to create a melancholy mood while the bow maintains continuity of sound.

M. 28-35 On the third beat of M. 28, the mood is very tranquil. At M. 30, play the 8th-notes very evenly and dryly, then create the rest of the phrase expressively. At M. 34, the 16th-notes are also dry and objective in character—geometrical.

M. 41-42 On the second beat, sing with a full sound, supporting this sound with a tightening of the diaphragm, the finger action deliberate, especially the fourth. Play as if each finger were reluctant to leave its note and move forward to the next.

M. 47-50 Create the 8th-notes almost flautato with the bow. Use this same color, very smooth, in M. 49. The next measure is more expressive in character.

Cadenza-Joachim

M. 77-79 The second sequence is a quiet answer to the first, which is singing in character.

M. 83-84 Hesitate slightly before resolving from the D sharp to the D natural; also from the F sharp to the F natural in the following measure. There is a poco allargando starting at M. 83.

M. 87 Play the repetitions of the double-stops (the first of each slurred group) deeper on the first three slurs, then play more evenly.

M. 92-93 Play quite dryly, phrasing after the E's on the first and second beats. On the fourth beat of M. 93, the character becomes more sustained.

M. 100 Play the two 16ths leading into the fermata very broadly.

M. 105-110 The first A is expressive, played with vibrato, the second pure, no vibrato, and the third almost disappearing. At M. 106, start to sing, initiating the first three 16th-notes with a small bow space, then using a proportionately larger bow space for the remaining 16ths. After the fermata at M. 108, the bow remains pianissimo through a slow deliberate shift to the higher A. The movement finishes as tranquilly as possible.

Andante Cantabile (♩=52-63)
Tutti
p
f p
f p
p
cresc.
f
p
Solo
sfp
sfp
(espress)
mp
mf
p
(dolce)
mf
cresc.
f
mp
(ma con suono)
sfp
sfp
tr
tr.
mp
mf
p

(Tutti)
*) Cadenza di Joseph Joachim
espr.
cresc.
dim.
calando
tempo
dolce
in tempo
ritenuto
poco - - - - - - - string
brillante
Tutti
espressivo
restez.
tranquillo poco rall.

RONDEAU

M. 1-4 This theme suggests a peasant dance, one with a slightly clumsy element and with a sort of dry humor. Play with very little vibrato, rather indifferently; finish the last 8th-notes of the phrase with no vibrato. Create each stroke in a controlled impeccable manner.

M. 6-13 Play this phrase more expressively. At M. 8, pull to the tip of the bow, hesitating before the G sharp, then repeat the opening theme in the same manner. At M. 13, play the last two 32nds more deliberately than the first two, then create the E in the following measure separately.

M. 15-24 To put the bow "on the track" for the short, fast strokes, play the first note, then "start" again on the second note. This phrase is played near the frog. Articulate the grace-notes with an almost pizzicato action in the fingers. At M. 18, initiate this phrase from the middle of the bow, so that the 8th-notes can be played near the tip very short, martellato. The forte-pianos in M. 23 and 24 should be played expressively in the left hand.

M. 32-41 After the two 8ths, stop to create the subito piano on the first note of M. 33. At M. 36, the first note is a fast stroke. Stop, then play the next stroke legato. From M. 37 through 41, play the 16ths in the middle part of the bow, then create a new face, flautato, pulling toward the point. return to the middle to initiate the following similar groups in the same manner.

M. 47-63 Play in a rhythmic, peasant-like manner; use a longer bow space for the 8th-note, playing this rather dryly. At M. 53 through 57, play the slurred 16ths with extraordinary finger action especially on the last two notes of each group, the bow "painting" pianissimo. At M. 60, the finger action must be more energetic in piano, taking care that the bow does not rush the fingers.

M. 101-107 Play the grace-notes on the beat, accenting them. Make a dramatic crescendo in M. 102 to prepare for the next passage. At M. 104, the last two 16ths of each group serve as an up-beat to the next; do not rush these.

M. 116 Stop after the first two 8ths and play the third short. Then create the following with a beautiful legato.

M. 125-154 Prepare for the Andante grazioso by making an allargando in M. 125, playing the final 8th-note D "long," then wait before playing the fermata D. The character of the andante is naive, peasantish: play this somewhat dryly. At M. 136, play in a more sustained manner, still dry in character. At M. 154, finish this section expressively, bringing out the A sharp.

M. 156 Initiate this section with a question-answer feeling on each group of four 16ths, taking care that the bow does not rush the fingers in the answer.

M. 165 Initiate the trills with a slight pinch in the bow, then cut the second note.

M. 175-177 Play more expressively through these measures, stopping the bow at the end of M. 177 before playing the final A.

M. 251 To accomplish the poco ritard, play the 16th-notes in M. 251 and 252 more deliberately. The bow spaces for the two final D's should be very exact.

Rondeau
Andante Grazioso (♩=63-80)
Solo
Tutti
Solo
Allegro, ma non troppo (♩.=ca.100)
(graz.)
leggiero
(graz.)

Andante grazioso
Tutti
Solo
Allegro, ma non troppo
cresc.
(legg.)
(dolce ed espr.)
Andante grazioso (𝅗𝅥=60-72)

148
mp
mf

155
(legg.)

159
espr.)

163
(mf)

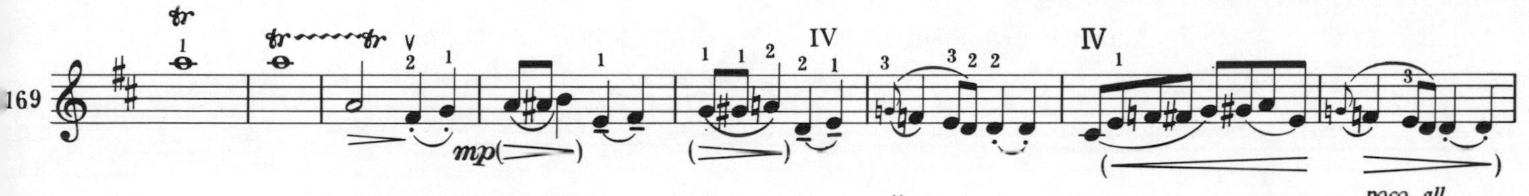
169
mp
poco all

Andante grazioso
177
(p.t.)

Allegro, ma non troppo
185
(f)

191
p

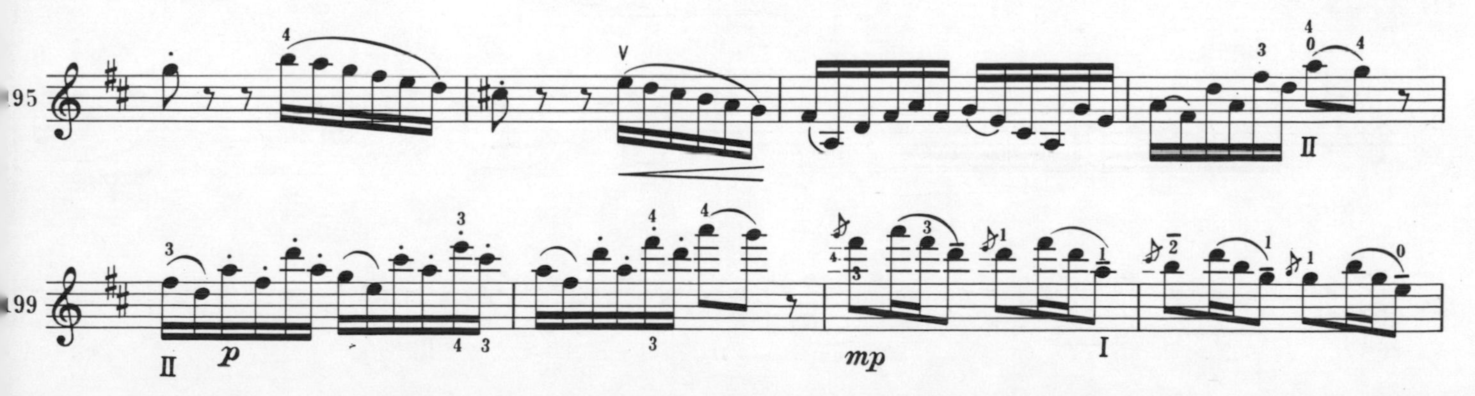
195
199
p
mp

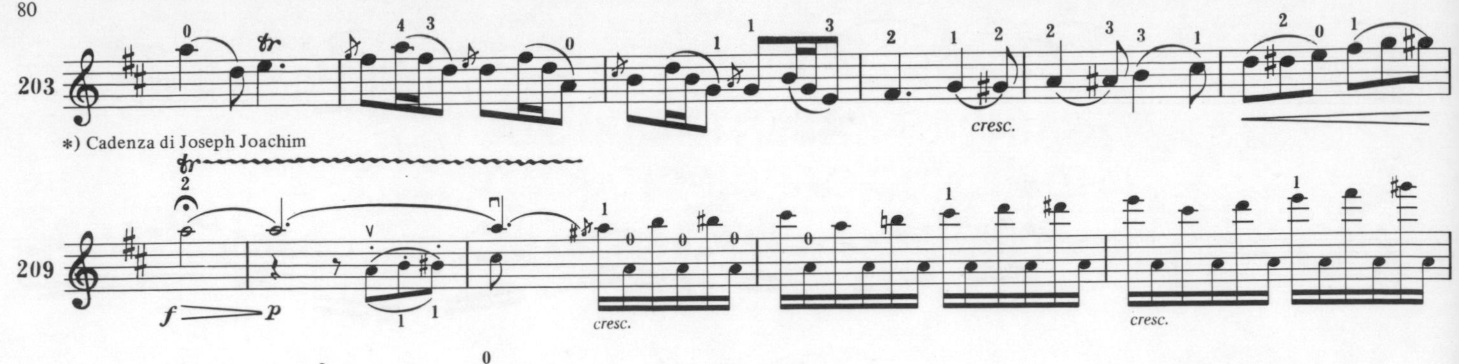
203
cresc.
*) Cadenza di Joseph Joachim
209
f
p
cresc.
cresc.

213
p
mf

poco ritenuto
l'istesso tempo
219
p

Andante grazioso
225
pp
pt.

Allegro, ma non troppo
232
fp
fp
fp

237
fp

242
cresc.

246
f
decresc.

250
p
poco rit.
pp

SAINT-SAËNS INTRODUCTION AND RONDO CAPRICCIOSO, OP.28

INTRODUCTION

There is a tradition of French elegance in Rondo Capriccioso which is typical of that school of playing which we inherited from Ysaye d Kreisler. This elegance is created within very compact spaces.

The typical violin concerto involves long elaborate musical lines; this piece is very concise and created through in impeccable left nd technique and controlled bow spaces. The vision created by the piece could be one of a circus. The introduction portrays a sad, trac clown or mime; the rondo depicts ballet dancers, jugglers, and acrobats; and the coda, announced by a suspenseful roll in the timpani, presents the grand finale with all of its color and fireworks.

.3-6 The first note must very expressive and the 32nd notes should have the feeling of pushing upward and forward to the F in M.4; is is also true of the next group of 32nd notes. Play tenuto on the A in M.5 and make a diminuendo to the E. The C is played elegantly, on e string in the lower part of the bow, and not too short. In M.6 play the D warmly with a big vibrato and make a crescendo.

.9 Play the G sharp—A expressively and the group of five notes in M.10 at the tip with a small bow space. Hold back on the last two otes.

.17 Play the B flat—G sharp with a deep bow and a deliberate feeling as this is the end of the section.

.20 The fast activity comes to an abrupt stop on the G sharp. From this note on play singingly; the same happens in M.24. At the end M.25 stop and create the new tranquil mood, then in M.26 each successive E should be played more tenuto.

32 Play this phrase broadly. In M.33 when the figure is repeated play the F a little longer and the C—D more deliberately. The trill-notes in Ms. 35-6 should get successively longer, and on the last three notes before the 6/8 play the A long and the G sharp—B fast.

40 Create each note individually and play with a short bow space. In M.41 make a stop then play the B warmly; do the same in M.43 the E. The F's in M.46 and 47 must be played long, not abrupt; there should be no roughness or pressing in the bow, almost like a brush oke. In M.48 play the A very short so there is time to get up to the E.

.54 As in Ms.46-47, here the E of M.54 and the B on M.55 must be held, not played abruptly. In M.57 play the last A expressively with notion.

.63 Play the harmonic A very short.

.72 At the tip, play the dotted 8th-note long and the 16th short, connected closely to the trill note. Accent the beginning of each trill making a slight pinch with the bow. The 16th-notes in M.75 should be played elegantly with no pressure. Stay in the upper part of the w except for the notes in the G string.

.80 The top E must be as short as possible.

.88 To make the staccato notes sound clearly, the left hand rhythm should feel as if it were anticipating the bow. In M.90 play immediately without waiting for the rest so that there is time to play the last notes without rushing. Make a slight break before beginning the ale in M.105; play the last three notes, B—C—D, sustained to re-establish the tempo for the theme.

.125 Subdivide the scale possibly on the second B, to maintain the rhythmic equilibrium, and play the last four notes more deliberely so that the end does not sound rushed.

.141-142 Play these two measures in the upper part of the bow. The high G, B, and D are short but the last G is more sustained and arming. The first three notes of M.143 should be played deliberately, the rest move ahead in tempo. In the second half of M.145 the ans-r should be played more tranquilly. From M.147 to M.150, beginning on the C sharp play each first note a little longer and in M.150 make proportional ritenute and diminuendo.

.152 Play this melody expressively with a singing tone but no special color.

.187-190 Watch that the last and first note of each group is clearly connected, being especially conscious of the rhythm so that the otes are not rushed.

.192 This is an echo of the previous measure, it should be played a little slower and pianissimo. To maintain rhythmic evenness do ot rush the note before the shift. Stop after the E in M. 193 and play the next three notes, E—G sharp—B, slowly; the next five notes, D arp—E—G sharp—B—D sharp, accelerando, and the last three allargando. M.195 should be played a little slower with a brushy spic-to and the first note of M.196 played tenuto. The glissando is played spiccato.

234 Make a slight break before the last note of the measure and ritard on the B—B flat. Play this melody like a slow waltz, use a lot bow-space and breathe freely. Pay special attention to the second notes so that they are not cut short. In M.242 play the last B a little ger to prepare for the next phrase. The 16ths in M.244 must be played deliberately and in M.246 the E flat must be very expressive. In 248 slow up on the last six notes. Play expressively and dramatically in M.251. In M.252 the first group accelerates and in M.253 make allargando.

255 To create the character of the upcoming phrase play the F expressively in the left hand, and pull lightly with the bow.

.304 The first chord of the cadenza is played tenuto; then play the next five chords in tempo with a feeling of moving towards the ord E—C—A which is played tenuto. The pattern is repeated as the next five chords are again in tempo moving to the chord A—F—E t. Both this chord and the next, B flat—F—D, are played tenuto. The next six chords beginning on G sharp—E—D are played poco ac-lerando, with a breathy laughing character. The last three chords of the measure should be played poco allargando. Make a slight break ter the last chord (D sharp—B—A) and play the last chord of the cadenza tenuto.

oda The timpani plays a suspenseful roll and the acrobatics begin. To maintain clarity and rhythm in the fast notes you should have e feeling that the left hand finger action is faster than the bow action (the left maintains rhythmic initiative and the bow follows).

Violin

A Monsieur Sarasate

et

RONDO CAPRICCIOSO

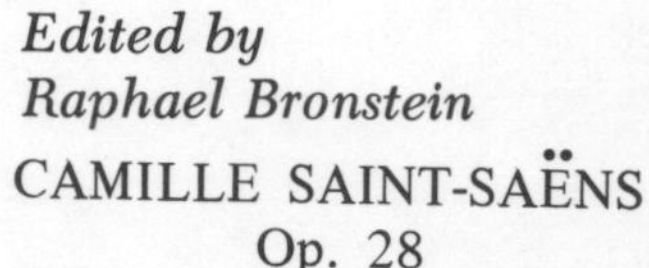

CAMILLE SAINT-SAËNS
Op. 28

Andante malinconico (♩ = 52)

sul G
II
III
IV
I
tr
p
40
46
51
57
63
69
74
79
83

III
tr
f
88

91
fp
f

94

97
restez.

100

B
103
f
p

106
sul G

112

118
cresc.

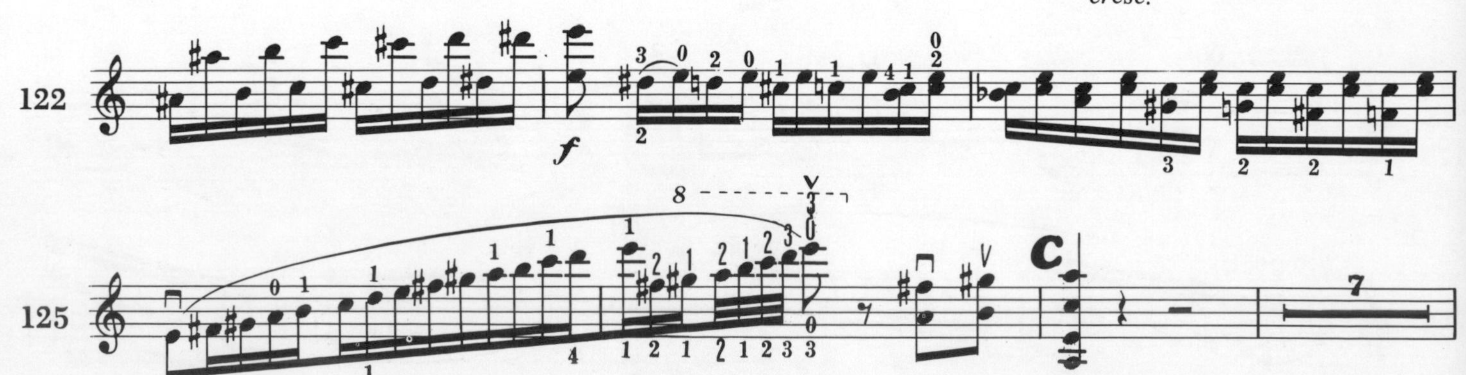
122
f
125
8
C
7

135
Pt.
sul G

140
IV
ten.
mp

144

147
dim.

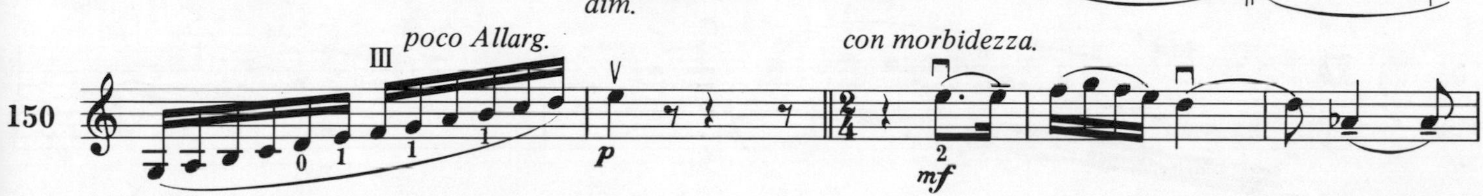
150
III
poco Allarg.
con morbidezza.

155
III
IV

163
III
IV
poco

170
a
poco
cres
cen
do

177

Tempo I.
183

86
Violin
dim.
gliss
ten.
D
sul G
cresc.
dim.
cresc.
cresc.

E
Pt.

dim.
espressivo

sul D

legg.
dolce
poco cresc.

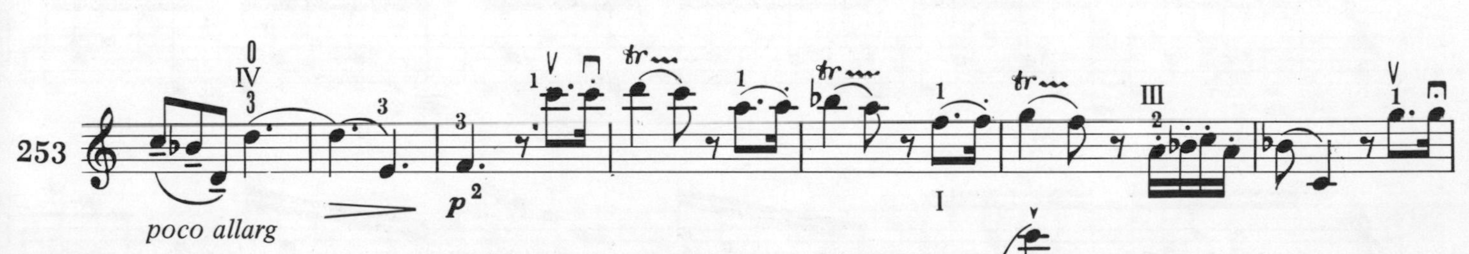
poco allarg

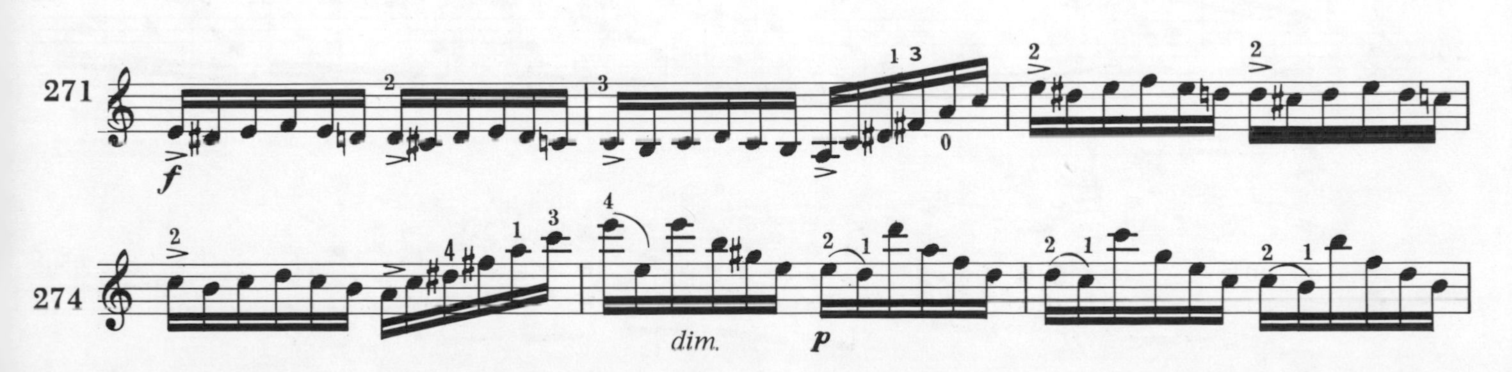
dim.

277
cresc.

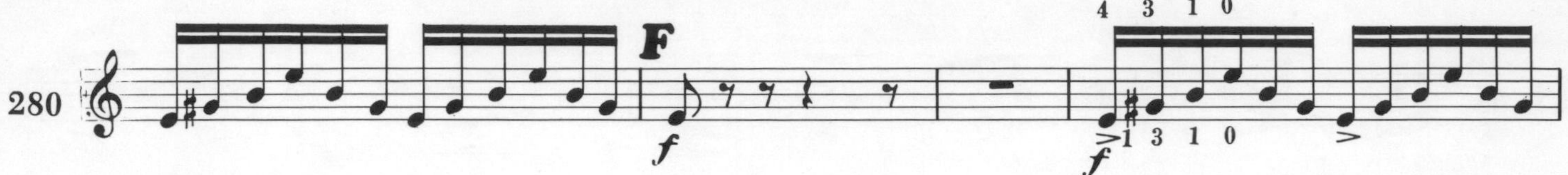
280
F
f
f

284
dim.
p

287

290

293

296
cresc.

299
f

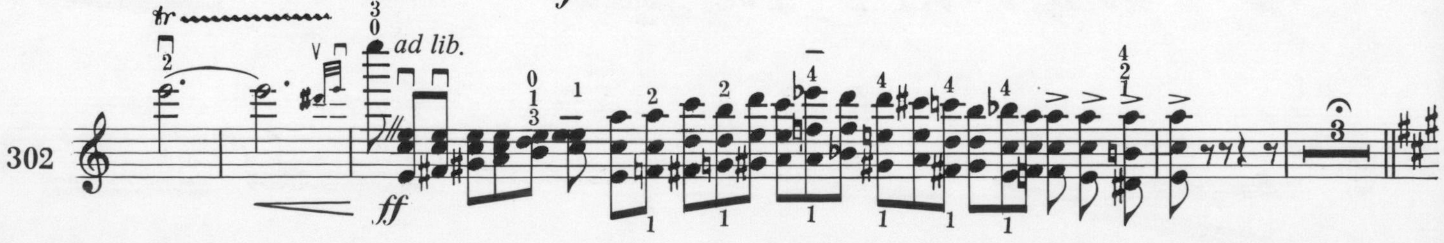
302
ad lib.
ff

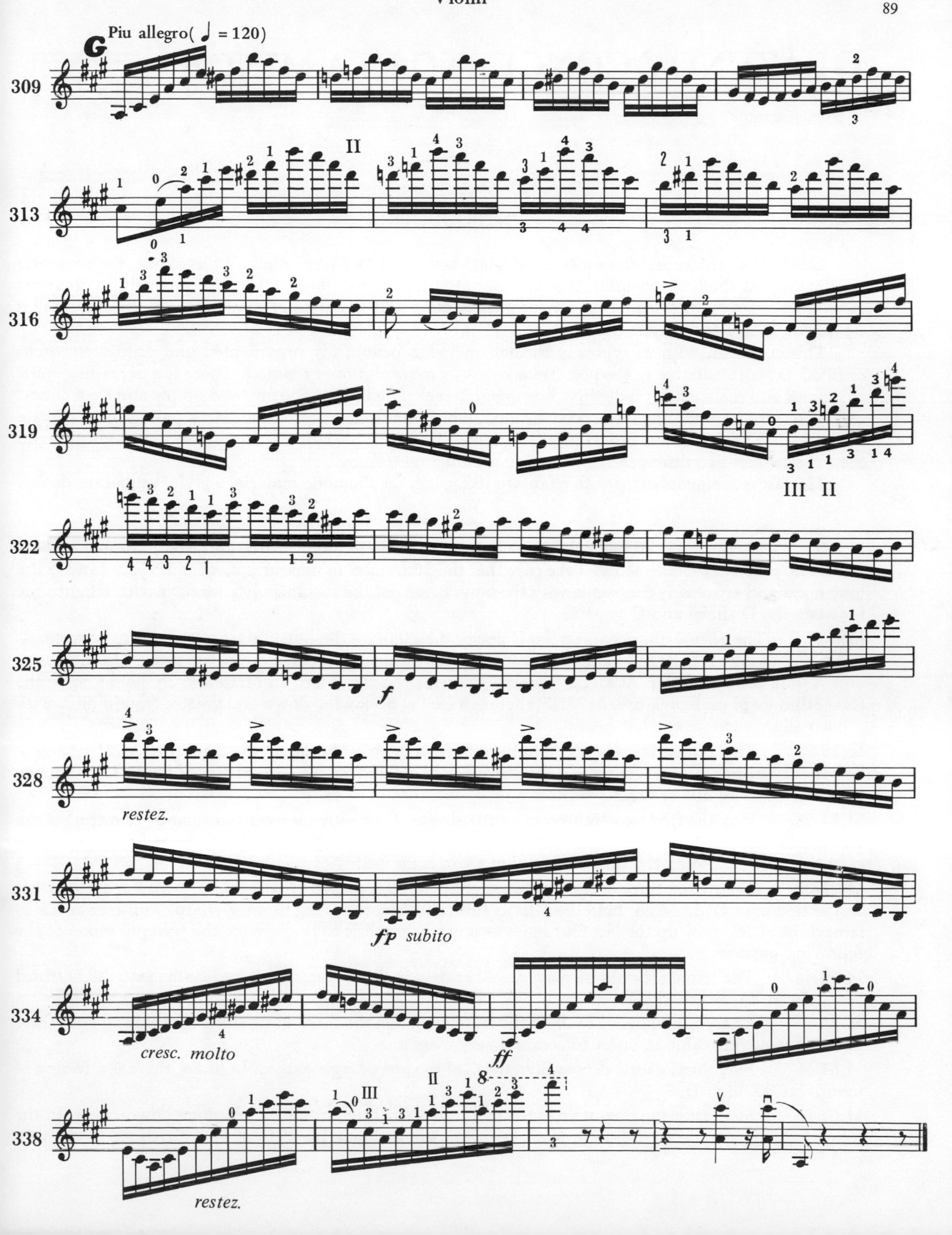
G
Piu allegro(♩ = 120)
restez.
fp subito
cresc. molto
ff
restez.

GLAZUNOV CONCERTO IN A MINOR

INTRODUCTION

One of the earliest performances of the Glazunov was with Efrem Zimbalist as soloist, the composer conducting. At the first rehearsal, they say that after the opening bars, Glazunov stopped the orchestra in wonder, so overwhelmed by the tender introspection and nostalgia of Zimbalist's interpretation that he asked, "Did I truly write this?"

This concerto, with its typically Russian melodies beautifully ornamented and exquisitely orchestrated, is representative of the post-Tchaikowsky pre-revolutionary period. There is a pervading spirit of sadness and melancholy in the first movement; a melody will start warmly and simply and then almost disappear into a wondering introspective mood, which in turn is transformed into a passage of desperate restlessness. The cadenza is beautifully fragmented in mood, phrases starting broadly, generously, and then chameleon-like disappearing into a questioning wistfulness.

The last movement begins with a fanfare-like spirit, the thematic material a joyful exuberant dance.

M.2-9 This phrase is all one color, mezzo-forte with no dynamic variation. Maintain a slow bow speed and play very connectedly. Take care that the 16th-notes in measures 2, 4, and 5 lean toward the long notes and are closely connected with the bow. Bring out the melancholy character with a light slide between the D sharp and C in M.2.

M.9-17 The phrase disappears on the G sharp, then initiate the next phrase with a lyrical sweetness. In M.10, hold the E to its full value (otherwise the third finger will come down too soon). On the harmonic A, pull the bow faster. At M.12, "spread" the stroke on the B flat. In M.15 and 16, hold long to the final 8th-note of each measure. At M.17, there is a feeling of slowing down and greater tranquillity, with a poco allargando on the last beat.

M.18-23 This phrase is energetic in nature. Spread the bow stroke on the final A of M.21 (the note before the harmonic). Use generous, long strokes in M.22 and 23. On the half-note C in M.23, change the tonal color to one of greater intimacy.

M.24-28 Play the first two 16th-notes a little slower, then move forward in tempo. The triplets are an imitation of the harp and should not be rushed. Play M.26 and 27 similarly. In M.28, take care to play the note preceding the shift well so that there is no feeling of rushing.

M.31-36 On the last three notes, slow up slightly. M.32 is played rhythmically, with a tenuto feeling on the tied-over D. In M.35, hold the F to its full value before sliding to the F sharp. This measure is in tempo. In M.36, slow up the last four notes as much as possible to prepare for the tranquil mood of the following passage.

M.42-44 The triplets should be played deliberately in the fingers, the bow leaning into the D (third beat). In M.44, make a rallentando.

M.52-53 There is a tendency to slight the second notes in the three-notes slurs; take care to hold these notes to their full value in order to create a very even line.

M.57-58 Play the C a little deeper than the C of the preceding measure. In M.58, there is a feeling of tenuto on the high D.

M.67-68 Stop after the final note of the run, then play the harmonics with long bow strokes. In the following passage, use small bow strokes, very compact and glue-like action, very rhythmic to the very end.

CONCERTO

VIOLIN

Edited by
Raphael Bronstein

Alexandre Glazounow Op. 82

Solo
31
p
mf

a piacere
34

a tempo
ma tranquillo
4
37
dolce, espressivo
p

animando
41

5
a tempo
44
f
poco rall.
dolce
II

47

animando
50
cresc.
f

calando
53
rit.

6
a tempo
56
mf
II
cresc.
8va

59
animando
cresc.

61
7 piu mosso
(♩=120)

63

65
poco dim.

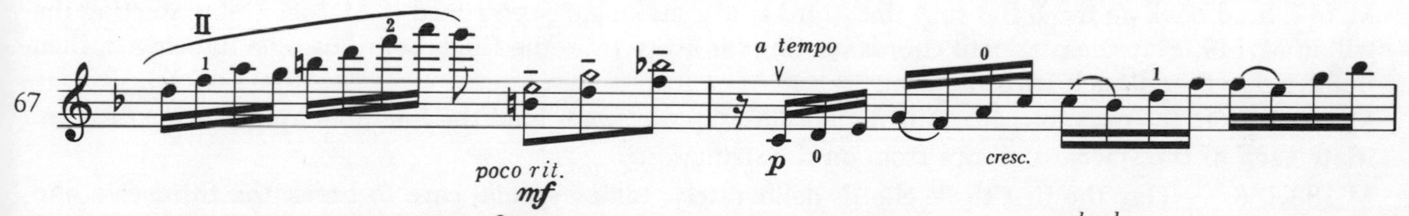
67
a tempo
poco rit.
cresc.

69
8va
Tutti
8 Tempo I
calando
(Celli e Bassi)

76
rall.
80
9 tranquillo
(Clar.)
(♩=76)
8va
Solo

83
rit.
vib.
poco cresc.

M.81-87 Remain on the C as long as possible to create a melancholy mood. The 16th-notes should not be rushed, but there must be a feeling of moving steadily forward from the third beat of M.83 to the second beat of M.84 where there is a feeling of holding back. At M.85, remain on the G very long, vibrating on the note an octave higher. On the second half of this note, the vibrato disappears, the mood more melancholic. Lower the finger for the A flat slowly, blurring the change, then let the bow remain on the string until after the tone has disappeared. Very slowly prepare for the down-bow to initiate the following section. This theme is beautifully lyrical, the vibrato constant and continuing with the same speed from finger to finger. The bow speed is even, taking care to use a small amount of bow on the last three 8th-notes of M.87 and with no feeling of rushing.

M.93-108 Play the A flat very warmly to prepare for the next phrase which is expressive and lyrical. In M.95, make a slide down to the F, playing pianissimo with the bow. On the A flat—A natural, play non-vibrato; use a small vibrato in the following two measures. M.98 is warm and expressive. M.99 is very expressive, almost desperate in the downward leap from A flat to B flat. The following measures are restless in nature with a feeling of moving forward. The last beat of M.107 is a preparation for the lyricism and sweetness of the next measures. Do not rush these last two double-stops.

M.114-117 This phrase is a melancholy echo of the preceding phrase. The 16th-note A should "lean" toward the harmonic D; then slide deliberately, "badly," from the harmonic. Play M.117 very expressively, using a very deliberate finger action with a slight tenuto on the B sharp.

M.122 The three-note slurs should be played with a small amount of bow, very even.

M.130-137 The first two measures are very expressive from the very first note, becoming increasingly melancholic in M.132 and 133. Hold the first notes of M.134, 5, and 6 long.

M.138-143 In the octave passage, concentrate on the singing quality of the notes on the A string. In M.140, play with a feeling of great tranquillity and with almost no vibrato. In M.142, count in 8th-notes for rhythmic steadiness and to maintain a feeling of slowness.

M.144-151 Play this passage with a strong finger action, preparing the finger well for the high D. at M.147, hold back on the B flat to A flat (third beat), making a poco ritard in M.148. Delay starting the trill in M.149. Play the pizzicato chords starting far away from the fingerboard using a flat finger, then pulling down and back with the arm.

M.168 On the two-note slurs, the fingers must "speak" well: hold the first note long, raising fast. Initiate each of the staccato groups from on the string.

M.183-186 Play the first three chords deliberately, taking special care to break the third two and two. Then move slightly faster, stopping before the final double-stop in this measure. Play this "long," then play energetically and fast on the two 16th-notes. M.185 is similar.

M.191 Take care to keep the bow strokes small on the 16-notes. There is a tendency to spread out on these which slows down the momentum.

M.207-208 Hold the harmonic D long, and play the D flat with a tenuto feeling. Beginning on the half-note low C, play this phrase like an echo; hesitate before the final note which disappears.

M.231 Play the last two 8th-notes deliberately, letting the high D sing; prepare the finger solidly before playing.

M.233-241 Hold the F harmonic quite long. In M.234, let this phrase sing straight-forwardly using generous fast strokes. The grace-notes are played deliberately and evenly. On the fourth beat of M.236, play the B quite long releasing the bow pressure, then play the C sharp alone mezzo-piano. Create the first part of M.237 very quietly, simply, dryly, remaining near the tip of the bow—a questioning reply to the first part of the phrase. Finish the F sharp, then prepare the bow on the string to initiate the following 16ths. Play these in a faster tempo, very rhythmic and dry in character. The phrase at M.238-241 is similar to the first, paying special attention to the even, deliberate grace-notes.

M.242 Play the quarter-note E and the following F with a tenuto feeling; let the final B of the measure sing long.

M.243-245 Play the second and fourth 16th-notes well on the fourth beat to bring out the melodic line of the lower voice. In M.244, play the last two 16ths in the first beat more expressively. In M.245, play the 8th-note tenths broadly.

M.250 At the piu sostenuto, play this theme with the same one-color as in the opening statement of the concerto.

andante (♩= 56)
10
86
IV
mf espressivo

92
III
II
p

11
98
cresc.
f passionato

103

107
12
p dolce
cresc.

agitato
13
f
p

cresc.

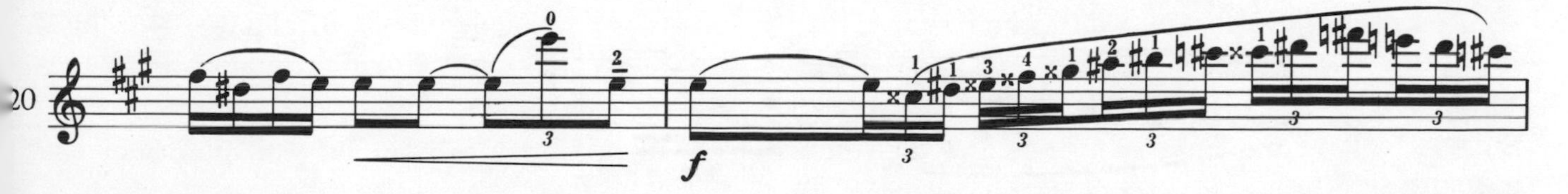
f

14

calando
124
dim.

126
p
poco allary
15
128
a tempo.
mf

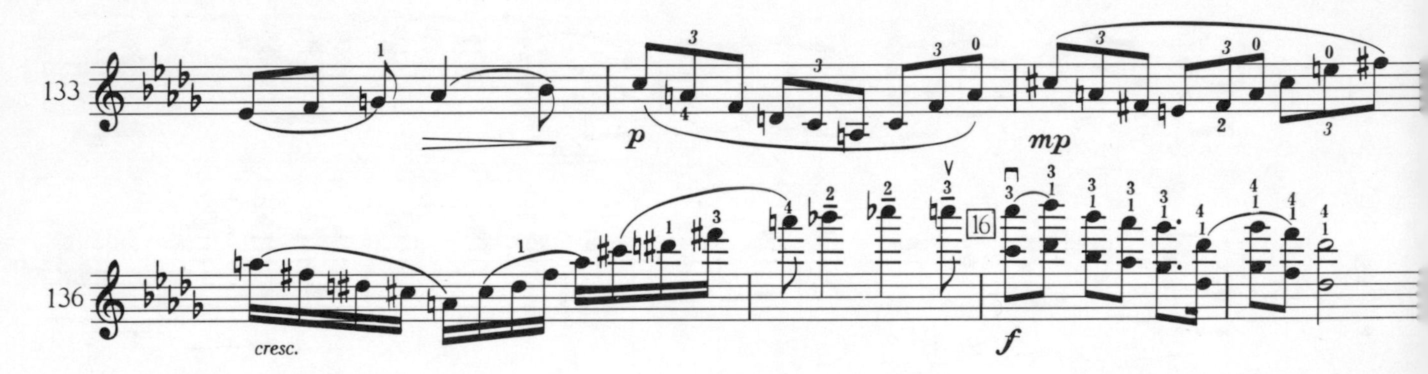
133
p
mp
136
cresc.
16
f

140
p
p
mf

8va
17
144
p piu tranquillo
dim.

147
pp

pizz.
18
Tempo I
a tempo
150
p
rit.
rit.

19
Tutti
a tempo
(Viol. I)
p
161
(Viol. II)
mf
(Fl.)
poco rit.

166
(Viol. I)
p
a tempo ma piu animato (♩=112)
20
Solo
mf
p

169
II

171
II

173

175
4 remain
II
I

21
177
mf
4 remain

179

181
pesante
(Viol. I)
22
f
Tutti
Solo
ff

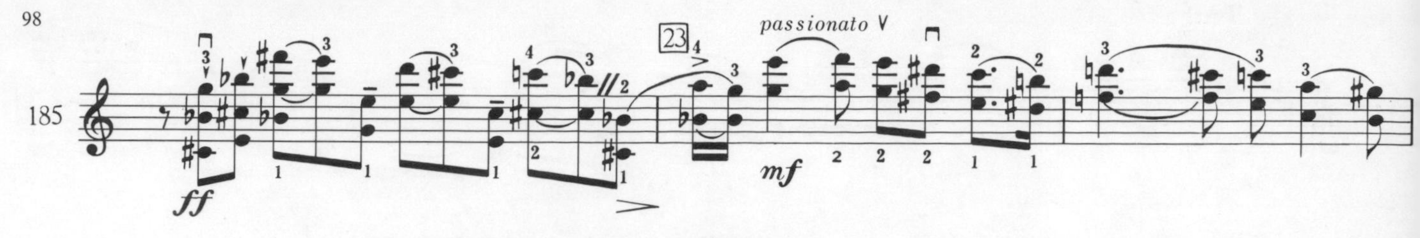
185
ff
23
passionato
mf

188
8va
a tempo
f

192
mf
pt.
24
p

195

198
cresc.
25
animato
f

202

205

207
poco allarg
Tutti
(Vcelli)
p
(viol. I)
mf
(Vcelli)
mf

tranquillo
IV
26 Solo
213
mf dolce

218
animando
sempre sul IV
rall.

27 a tempo
221
III II

animando
IV
226
cresc.
f
poco rit.

8va
a tempo
230
mf
28
f

Cad. a piacere
233
poco rit.
II
mf
III
p

II
237
pp
p
mf

ten.
II
240
p
pp
mf

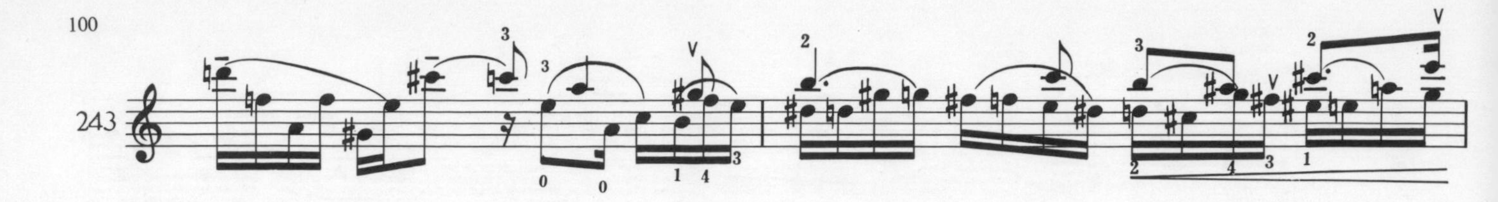
243

245
ten.
dim.

247
8va
poco rit.
pizz.
piu
arco.

sostento
251
IV

255

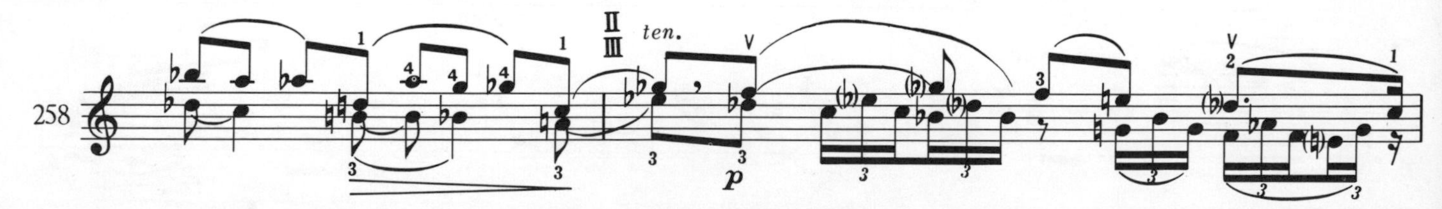
258
II
III
ten.

260

I
262

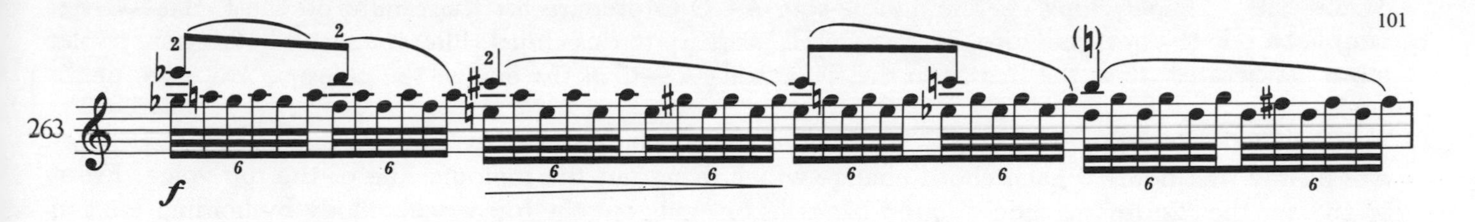
263

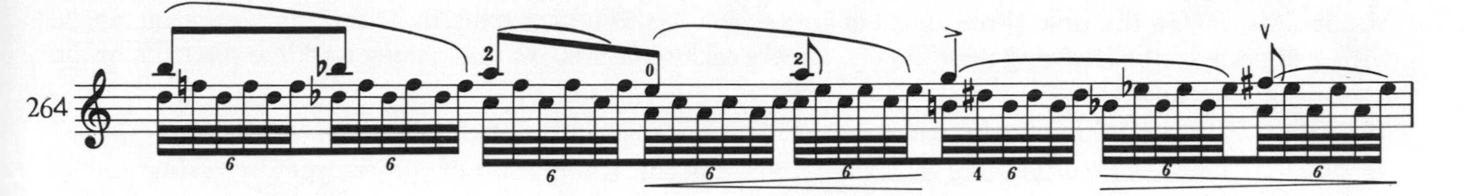
264

II & III
265

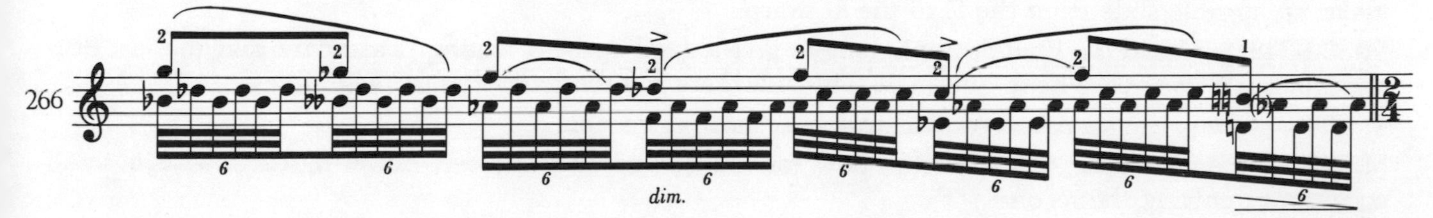
266
dim.

29
animando
PT.
267
cresc.
269
remain
dim.

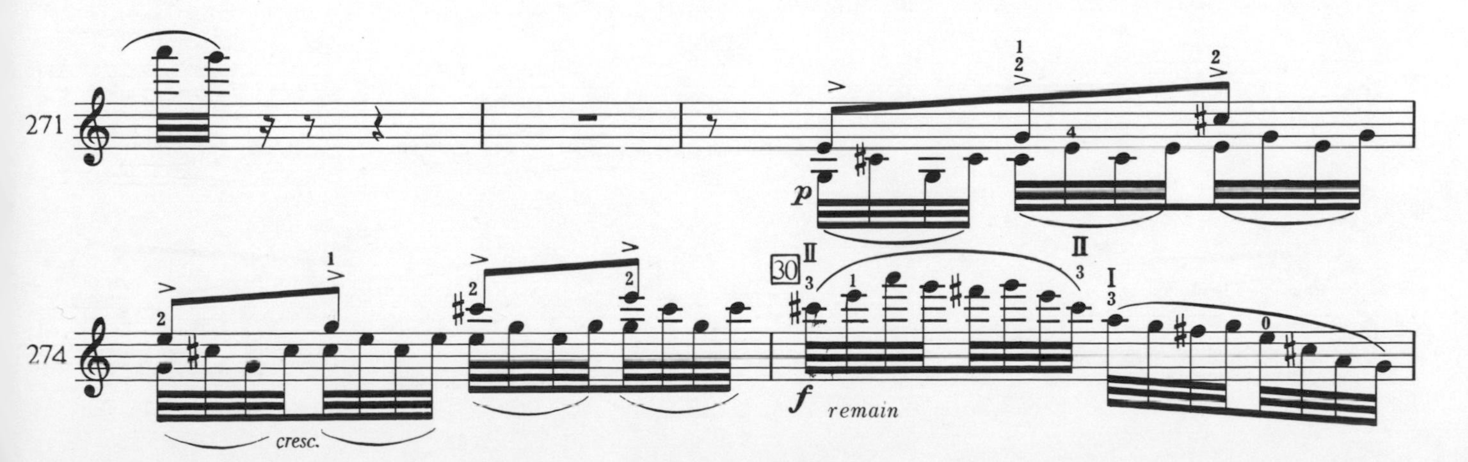
271
274
cresc.
30
remain

M.258-259 Hold "long" to the double-stop A—C to prepare for the tenuto on the E flat—G flat double-stop in the next measure. Make a "tired" slide up to this chord. Play the second 16th-note triplet more deliberately than the first; also the E natural—G—C at the end of the measure are more deliberate.

M.261-263 Play the final F in M.261 long to give a good up-beat feeling into the next passage. Vibrate on the first notes of each chord change which bring out the melodic line of the top voice. From M.263 on, the 32nd-notes should sound like trills bringing out the top voice melody by holding long to the first notes before beginning to trill.

M.266-268 On the final three chord changes, slow up to a lazy trill. In M.267, initiate each stroke with a slight accent remaining near the tip. Create each separately so that they sound like the trills in the preceding passage.

M.283 Hold on to the final harmonic until the entrance of the trumpet, then cut.

M.288 Maintain a fanfare-like character, imitating the articulation of the trumpet by taking special care to play the 16th-notes very short.

M.305-308 Make the connection from the 16th to the following 8th-notes very close (a short note should "lean" toward the long). At M. 308, remain near the tip of the bow.

M.324-325 This section is slower in tempo, lyrically expressive. Take care that the 16th is very short, the following 8th held long.

M.331 There is a feeling of holding back in this measure; hold the D long.

M.335-339 Vibrate through the shifts (C sharp—B, M.335-6; A—G sharp, M.337). In M.338-9, make an audible slide from the E to the D sharp.

M.339-342 Hold the final 8th-note long to give a good up-beat feeling. Take care that the last 8th-notes of each stroke are held long in M.340-342; there is a tendency to cut these notes.

M.366 Keep the successive down-strokes as short as possible.

M.390 Remain near the tip of the bow for the slurred 16th figures, initiating each with a small accent and cutting the second 16th.

M.398 Hold the first note of each stroke before starting the tremolo.

M.406 Keep the bow on the string in the upper part throughout this passage.

M. 494-497 Stop the bow after the final 8th-note of each measure and prepare the fingers well on the first of each.

M.541-543 To create the diminuendo and to prepare for the following passage, use less bow space for each stroke. From M.544 it is permissible to accelerate to the very end.

M.587 The octaves are more effective than harmonics.

276
dim.

278
mp
cresc.

280
f
dim.

8va
282
p
cre
scendo

31
allarg. (♩= 84)
284
marcato
Solo
f
marcato

32
(Trombe)
289
f

Solo
293
f

PT.
33
298
p

* Pizzicato with left hand

329
37
a tempo
a piacere
p
cresc.

334
f
p

38
quasi allegretto ed espressivo
339
mp

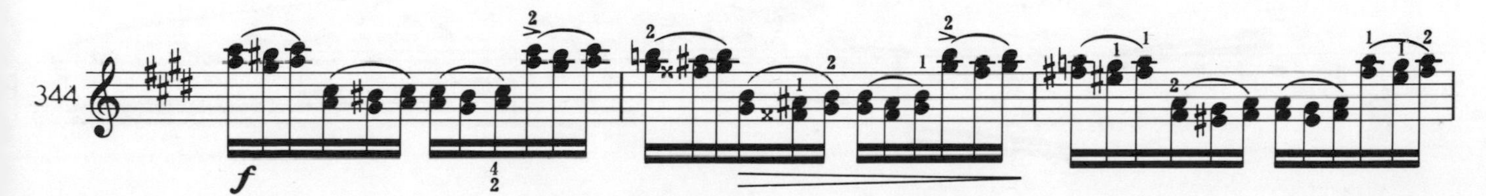
344
f

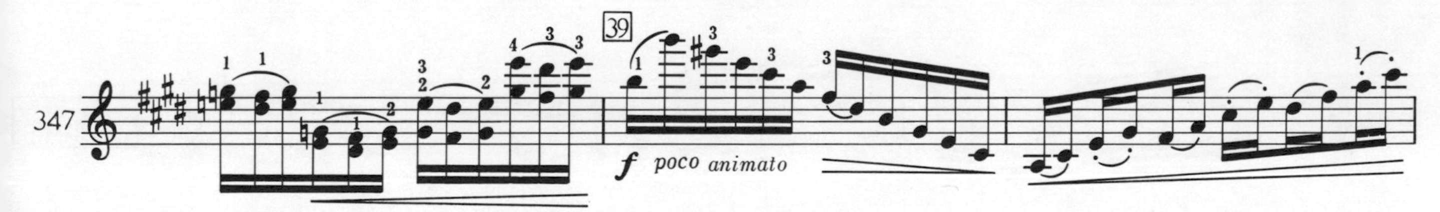
39
347
f
poco animato

354
f

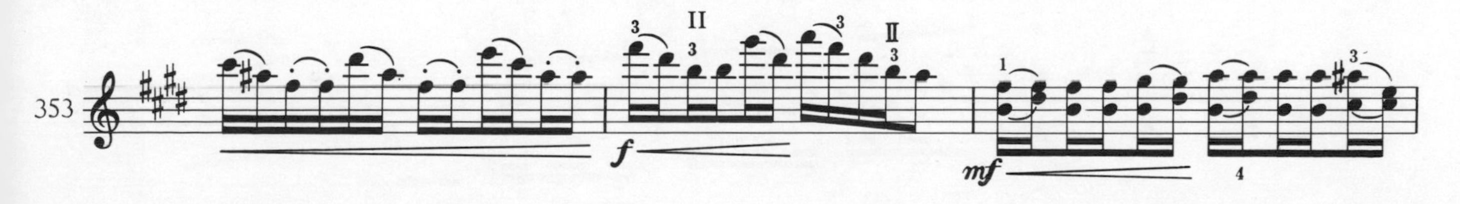
353
f
mf

Tutti
40
356
f
ff

360
IV
Solo

41
366

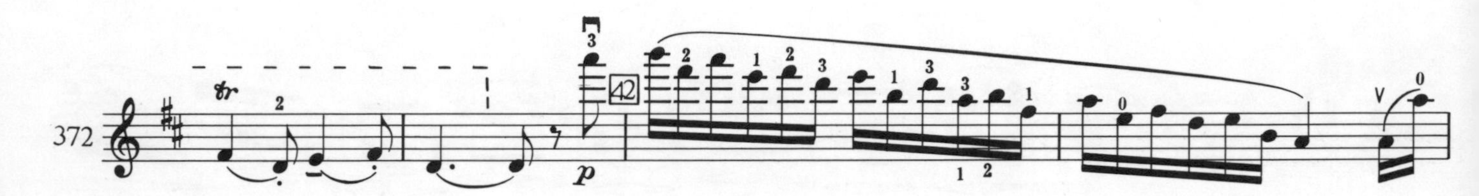
372
42

376

379
IV

43
Tutti
(Viol. I)
382

389
Solo
44
pt.

393

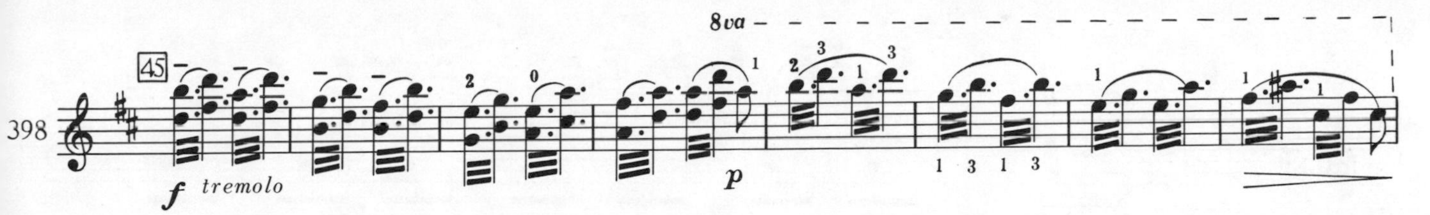
8va
45
f tremolo
p

PT.
mf
cresc.

46
IV
ff
ff
f

IV
47
Tutti
corni IeII
animando poco a poco
mf

Solo
p dolce
mf

48
p
sempre animando

piu animato (♩=138)
49
mf
pt.

50
cresc.
ff tr
tr

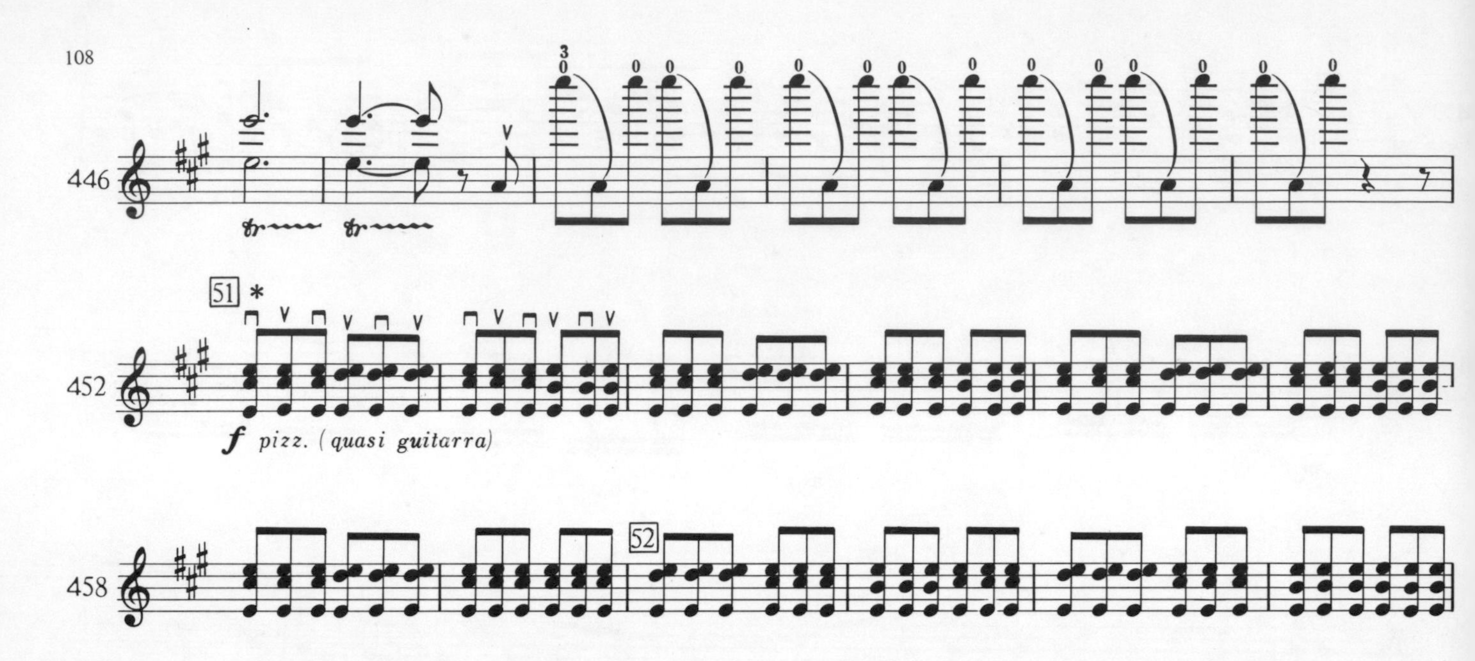

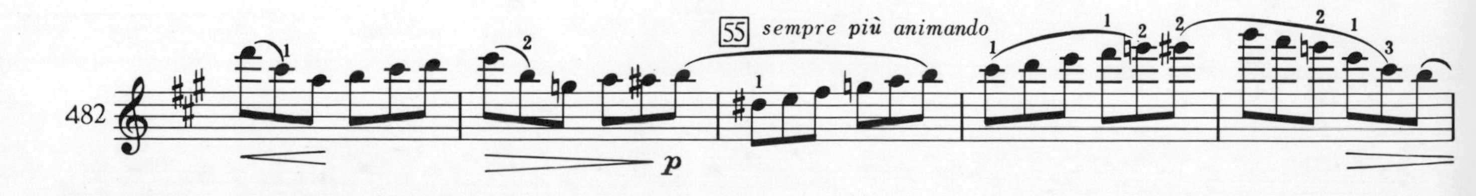

*In this case the ⊓ and V signs designate the down-and up-stroke of the right-hand first finger for the pizzicato chords.

492
mf
mf
IV
cresc.

(♩= 160)
56
496
III
I
f

501
II
I
II
f

506
IV
cresc.
II
I
f

(Viol. I)
57
511
8va
Solo
ff
f
mf

516
Tutti
(Viol. I)
Solo
8va
Tutti
(Viol. I)
f
mf
f

58
Solo
522
segue
f
mf
mp

528
f

59
534
mf
sempre animando
ff

540
dim.
60
p

546
cresc.
61
f

552
dim.

62
558
p
cresc.

564
f
63
f

571
Solo
mf
f
Solo
mf

578
ff
64
f
ossia
pf

584

CHAUSSON POÈME, OPUS 25

INTRODUCTION

Chausson's Poeme is a story of tragedy and desperation which must be presented with a feeling of tenderness, characteristics all typical of the French school. In writing this piece, which expresses great lyricism and self-pity, Chausson was inspired by the story of "May Nights" written by Nikolai Gogol which describes ghost tales of the Russian peasantry. He was deeply affected by the tremendous variety of moods depicted in the horror tales which presented elements of restlessness and at the same time poetic tenderness.

The opening solo should be played as if one were searching for a theme, as legend has it that Chausson and Ysaÿe did in composing the improvisational introduction. The melodic ideas are only embryonic, not clearly defined. Each note should be played with no anticipation of what is to come so that the listener feels as if the performer is truly improvising.

With Chausson's permission, Ysaÿe rewrote the section shown below, and performed the Poème in the revised form.

M.31 Lean on the first note without making an accent, then release the bow pressure by relaxing the arm. In M.36 the B flat should speak warmly because it is the arrival point of the previous two measures. Play M.37 with the feeling of moving forward and M.38 holding back. Use a small bow space on the F and decrescendo towards the E flat. The B flat of M.40 begins a new phrase so it should have a well defined sound.

M.42 The G flat and A flat should be played tenuto and connected. Vibrate through the shift.

M.47 On the second half of the B flat the color becomes more passionate. Grow in intensity through the next two measures then vibrate through the shift to the A—E flat of M.49. In playing the chord of M.50 the bow crossing should be deliberate with a slow forearm motion to give the chord a rounded sound. In M.51, when the B flat is played alone, move the finger back to play a little flatter.

M.65 Each time delay starting the trill and stop it on the third beat. The runs should be played deliberately.

M.69 These measures must be played solidly. On the up strokes play the second notes of each group more expressively by using a long bow space on that note. M.71 should be played in tempo but with a feeling of forward motion to the B flat of M.71. Again, in M.71, play solidly paying special attention to the second notes of the slurs. Hold back in M.72 on the last two notes and make a break before M.73.

Dedicated to EUGÈNE YSAYE

POÈME

VIOLIN

Edited by
Raphael Bronstein

ERNEST CHAUSSON, Op. 25

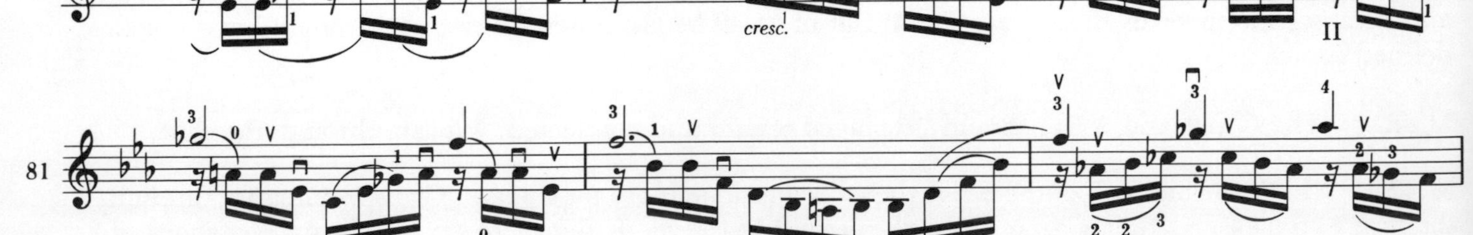

M.73-75 The down-bows should be played into the string using a lot of hair and an even long bow stroke; play towards the bridge. The up-bows are played flautato with a very light fast bow on the F just touching the B natural.

M.76-79 In M.76 make a proportional ritenuto and diminuendo. The last note is held long and played dryly, then hesitate before going on. In M.77 with a light bow play the long notes beautifully and the 16ths evenly and pedantic. Before the E flat in M.78 stop a little to set the bow, then paint with an airy bow stroke. In M.79 play broadly, evenly, and into the string.

M.80-84 Sing on the top note, especially in Ms.81 on the G natural and 82 on the F. In M.83 watch that the second note of the 16ths is not rushed. Play with a feeling of moving forward in M.84, then holding back in M.85.

M.87-90 Play heavily with great conviction and intensity, almost screaming the notes. The character becomes more dramatic in M.89; hold out the last three notes to lead into the chord of M.90. Play the E flat of the chord long then move to the top note, F sharp, and hold it. This note should be played with a passionate vibrato which continues through the shift with the fourth finger.

M.96 Hold the top B flat long then in M.97 move in tempo.

M.102-105 On the second half of the C flat diminuendo to piano, then die away using a smaller bow space on each note. Slide into the last B flat of M.105.

M.113 This should be beautifully expressive playing; be sure all the measures are very connected and watch to avoid accents at the top and the frog. The bow distribution should be very even and all the notes held out to their full value.

M.127 The character here becomes more intimate.

M.135 Move forward on the D—C, hesitate on the C, then play so that the notes are "patched" together (connected). On the F—D hold back and play quietly. Hold back in M.136 on the D—C but play intensely with a very connected feeling. The D—E flat in M.136 is played deliberately and into the string. In M.137 the F—E flat should cry, then die away.

M.138-142 Play with a feeling of moving forward but in a steady tempo. In Ms.140 and 142 the third finger vibrato should continue through the shift while the bow action is very connected. The character in M.145 is very dramatic.

M.149 Stop at the end of the measure and prepare both the left and right hands for the G of M.150. In M.151 stop to prepare the shift to the last A, finish the last four notes well, then play the last D.

M.164 After the 8th note play the first two 16ths deliberately, accelerate slightly up to the last two 16ths and play these deliberately, after the next 8th note stop and begin the pattern again. Use the upper half of the bow with a horizontal bow stroke using the whole arm and moving from the shoulder.

M.168 The first note is played with the bow on the string, then play with a brushy spiccato close to the string in the lower half of the bow. When a note is repeated, as in M.171, play the second note more intentionally and deliberately.

M.172 Using a small arm motion begin in the lower half of the bow and play very controlled. In M.173 when shifting from F—D flat to B flat—D flat stop the bow before the shift and prepare the fourth finger for the next note. The last note before the octaves in M.179 is an important upbeat; use a fast bow stroke and connect the note to the following octaves. In playing the octaves sing on the bottom note and don't place too much emphasis on the E string.

ten.
ff
Animato
ff
dim.
p tranquillo
f
sul A
sul D
p
cresc.
p
f
ff
Molto animato

M. 192-197 Play with a generous amount of bow on the first of the slur, then for the rest of the phrase on each bow stroke slow the speed and use less space. In M. 197 the last three notes are played quietly and dryly with no expression.

M.204 The first group is played deliberately and in tempo, then become proportionally slower on each successive group, hesitating slightly before the last note.

M.215-223 Play the D flat with a flattened third finger, then round the finger and play more on the tip by moving the hand forward for the D natural. In M.216, to create the necessary intensity, play into the string. Move forward in M.218 and in M.223 make a ritard.

M.225-236 Play with a sweet tone and great expression without forcing the bow. Intensify the expression on the A in M.234 and again on the D in M.236.

M.239 Make an allargando and stop before the 6/8. M.240 is played in tempo with a large bow space. On each succeeding up-bow play with a forward feeling. On each group of notes from M.244-246 push towards the top note then play tenuto on the last.

M.253-259 To make the crescendo play each note slightly deeper and longer. Use a large bow space on the first note of each slur. On the last up-bow of M.254 decrescendo. In M.255 the bow space and speed should be evenly distributed and in M.259 play more deeply into the string.

M.270-305 After making a slight ritard in M.270 using a small bow play piano; the mood should be restless. In Ms.294 through 301 the last note in each group is played tenuto and must scream. The theme in M.305 must be a continuation from the orchestra. Play with a full vibrato to create a large tone.

M. 316 The last two E flats should prepare for the tranquil mood of the top B flat. To give the B flat a secure sound stop after the E flats and set the fourth finger firmly on the note, then play.

M. 318-322 Hesitate on the E flat, make a ritenuto, and disappear. The character of the last two notes, B flat and G, should be very tragic and pathetic. In M. 319 play evenly, and in M. 326 with a feeling of slowness. Begin a ritard in M. 323, and in M. 326 crescendo to the B flat of M. 327. "Fall" on this note, then diminuendo; the note should be played tenuto, as if not wanting to go on. The up-bow in M.328 is played dryly.

M. 330-334 Play in tempo at first then ritard slightly on the second group. The last group must be slower, singing and emotional.

M. 341 Between each note through M.344 make a slight separation. Beginning on the first A flat of M. 343 start to ritard. The last A flat of M. 344 should be played with a slow lazy trill, and the last note, G, should die away while the bow pulsates on each beat. This ending should be reminiscent of a leaf falling or a bird flying with a broken wing. All the nightmares and moodiness disappear in the pathetic mood.

EDITORS NOTE

The following are corrections which Chausson made in collaboration with Ysaye after the first publication:

15 bars after number 4—omit the B flat in the last beat.
6 bars after number 11—the 1st double-stop is C-G not A-G.
14 bars after number 11—A natural in the first triplet and A sharp in the third triplet.
1 bar before number 12—A sharp in the second triplet.
Number 20—last beat D natural and C natural descending, C sharp and D sharp ascending.
2 bars after number 20—in the last beat, D natural and C natural descending, C sharp and D sharp ascending.

Animato (aTempo)
mp (flottato)
mf
f
ff
sul G
rit.
Poco Lento
p
riten
Poco lento
sul D
mf
string.
poco
poco rit.
Poco meno lento

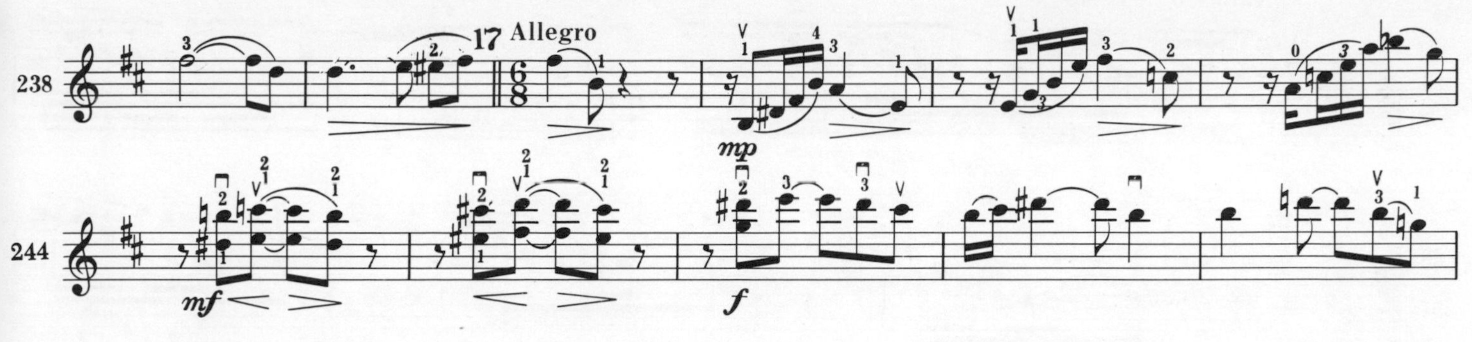
17 Allegro
mp
mf
f

cresc.

18
p
f
mf
19
accel.
cresc.
20
ff
restez
sfz

294

297

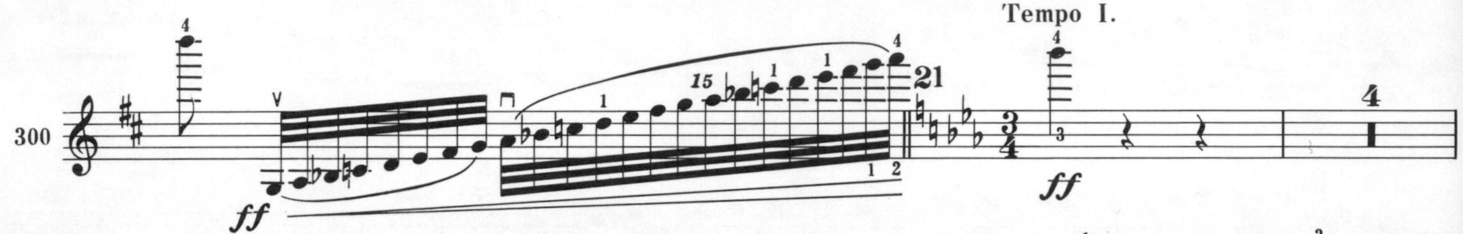
300
ff
21
Tempo I.
ff

306
mf

312
pp

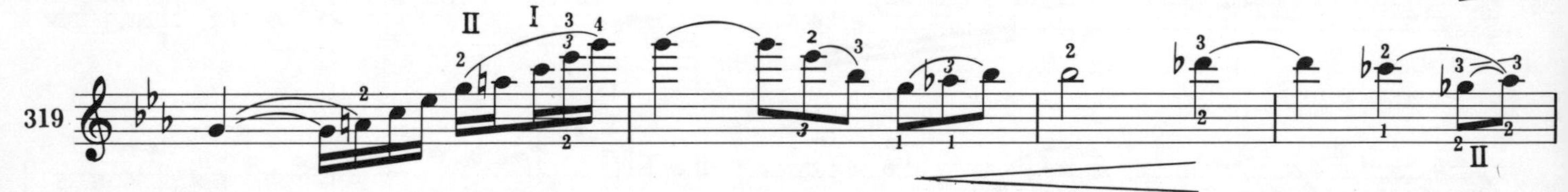
319

323
crescendo
22
p

330
335

342
rit.

SIBELIUS CONCERTO IN D MINOR OPUS 47

INTRODUCTION

From the very first note of this concerto we are in the nordic world of fiords, woods, and white nights. Sibelius is the last of the great romantics, but more significantly his works are a reconfirmation of the legends and sagas so deeply ingrained in the Nordic culture. He is preoccupied with the faces of nature rather than with people. He conjures up detached pictures of nature—the serenity of water and woods, the awe of rocky heights, and the brooding mysticism these inspire.

This concerto is made up of a sucession of pictures—a swan moving on serene waters, a light-house with the reflection of its light on the water, of legendary giants throwing rocks and thunderbolts with all the abandon which is possible in a land where the people live closely to and are emotionally deeply affected by the forces of nature.

The bow "paints" the faces of nature, the fingers "speak", in creating the kaleidoscopic moods and colors in this work.

FIRST MOVEMENT

MEASURE 4-13 The serenity of the orchestral introduction suggests that of a calm lake. The violin entrance should not disturb this calmness. It could be likened to a swan which does not disturb the surface of the water it swims over. Play with a tranquil bow action, the vibrato warm but small. On the harmonic A, use a very small bow space near the tip; the following D is especially tranquil. The triplet 16th-notes in M.7 are not very fast. At M.8 and 9, the character becomes sweet and smooth with no color changes in the bow and no crescendo. Use a very small amount of bow for the 16th-notes and play them very evenly.

MEASURE 14-24 The first sign of agitation begins here. At M.17, the swan disappears and the character becomes dramatic, restless, with a feeling of moving forward. Hold the high E in M.17 long—also that in M.19. In M.20, sing almost desperately, cryingly, the 8th-notes played very dramatically. In M. 22, make a slide from the F to the B flat playing this note with a great intensity. The E flat in M.24 should disappear.

MEASURE 25-32 The 16th-notes lean toward the following longer notes. Keep the bow space small on these 16ths.

MEASURE 33 There is a tendency to cut the low D short. Hold this note as long as possible with a feeling of length in the bow.

MEASURE 35-40 The 16th-notes should not sound rushed; play the B flat well before the shift. In M. 36, create the fz with a more intense vibrato rather than with a bow action. In M.37, play the 8th-note D deeper (in general, repeated notes should be played "better"). In M.40, vibrate energetically on the high B flat; do not force with the bow.

MEASURE 41-43 This passage suggests the violence of the force of nature—of rocks being thrown. Play with strong finger action and strong accents in the bow on the first and third beats of M.42.

Dedicated to Franz von Vecsey

CONCERTO

for Violin and Orchestra

VIOLIN

I.

Edited by
Raphael Bronstein

JEAN SIBELIUS, Op. 47

Allegro moderato 𝅗𝅥=54-60

MEASURE 49-51 Accelerate in the second half of this measure. Hold the high E long, then cut. The first two chords on the second beat of M.51 are deliberate and slow, then accelerate slightly. The string crossings are rapid, played like broken chords.

MEASURE 53-57 Remain in the lower part of the bow for this passage, but with no application of pressure. The finger action is energetic. In M.56, the thumb becomes an obstacle in the shift to the A; to compensate for this obstacle, feel high on the A, and feel low on the following C natural.

MEASURE 59-70 Cut after the E flat. Play the third and fourth notes of each 16th-note group very roughly. As this passage accelerates, do not worry about playing each note separately—it should begin to sound like double-stops. At M.70, play each note singly again, slowing up slightly before Tempo I.

MEASURE 71-75 Hold the E slightly longer, then proceed strictly in rhythm, sustaining the high D in M.75 as long as possible.

MEASURE 98 The clarinet sings a plaintive motive which evokes a feeling of something beautiful lost. In M.99, use a slightly longer bow space on the D; do not rush the E flat—E. This section suggests a picture of a light-house. The repeated note F is like the reflection of light on water, each one created with less bow. Stopping after the final F, create the B to harmonic D; the light disappears on this harmonic.

MEASURE 101 Prepare the bow on the string before playing the arpeggio and play with a solid glue-like action, the wrist firm and a feeling of weightiness in the fore-arm. The up-beat double-stop into M. 102 should be substantially played, not too short. The second double-stop in M.102 should be played with a slower bow speed to achieve a feeling of "spread" in this passage. In the octave passage (M.105) almost ignore the E—string notes, singing on the A—string.

MEASURE 108-115 Play with a compact bow space, deeply, so that the intensity of the long A flat in M.109 will not be lost. In M.112, use a long flautato stroke on the D flat—A flat; hold the final A flat "long". Disappear on the A flat of M.113, stop, and initiate the next passage with deliberate slow strokes. The first three are slower, stopping after each, the next three are slightly faster, the next three slightly slower. Hold the high A flat as long as possible.

MEASURE 116-119 This passage almost cries. Slide without vibrato from the last note of this measure to the F to achieve a plaintive sound. There is a feeling of moving forward up to the fourth beat of M. 117, then hold back for two beats, holding the E flat long, then move forward to the trill.

MEASURE 122-127 Jerk each note even if it means stopping the bow for each one. Change bow on each accent if necessary in order to achieve this action. At M.123 and 4, the two quarter notes are equal in bow space. The phrase which is initiated by the chromatic run should be played roughly. The grace-notes which lead into the Allegro molto should be played very deliberately.

MEASURE 222-227 Stop the bow before playing the high B flat. Play the B flat in the next measure with a tenuto feeling, and initiate the first three 16th-notes with a deliberate action. On M.224 move strictly in tempo. The arpeggio in M.226 is beautiful, lyrical in character; vibrate on the top G's of M.226 and 227.

MEASURE 230 Glue the short notes to the following long notes with a very close action.

50
(gliss)
ten.
a tempo
veloce
ff
mf

54

ma poco a poco crescendo
Largamente
ten.
57
f
mf

poco string
60
cresc. poco a poco

63

66
ff

Tempo I
Clar.
69
poco
allarg.
segue

72
crescendo

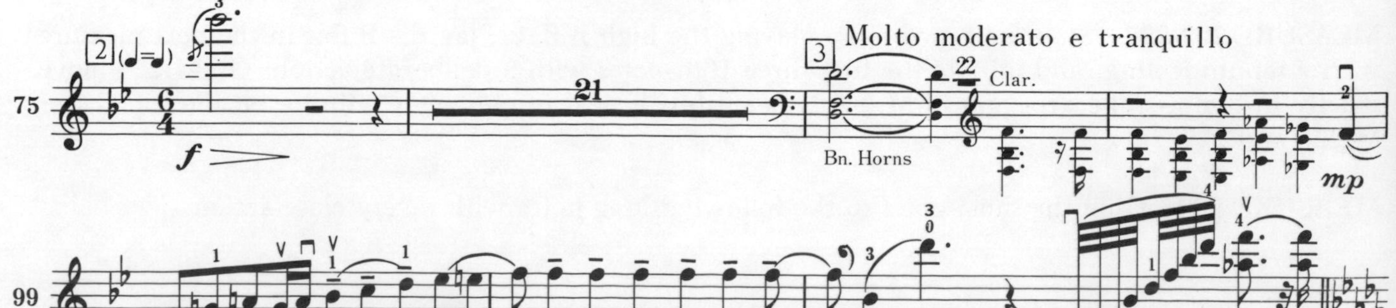
Molto moderato e tranquillo
75
21
22
Clar.
Bn. Horns
f
mp
99
poco f

Largamente
espress.
f affettuoso
mf
mp
p
diminuendo
Poco a poco meno moderato
dim.
crescendo
Allegro molto
Moderato assai
sempre
Cadenza

MEASURE 234-237 Break the chord two and two, then let the A continue alone. The 16th-notes begin slowly, then move in tempo at M.235. The run in M.237 should be in tempo, taking care not to rush, especially the last eight notes.

MEASURE 241-248 Sing deliberately on the E—F sharp—G, then continue without stopping through to the rest in M.244. The next phrases are similar in character; hold the fermata quite long. Play the next two measures very deliberately; the 16th-notes are dramatic in character and should be played substantially.

MEASURE 249 The triplets should feel slow. Each note of the arpeggiated chord should be heard separately as the bow crosses from string to string concentrating on a good horizontal movement. Hold the first chord long, recovering very quickly for the second chord; this one is also held long, then let it disappear.

MEASURE 251-254 This phrase is innocent in character; play it in tempo, using a small amount of bow. On the fourth beat, play deeper and slower. On the fourth beat of M.252, play even deeper and slower, very deliberately. On the fourth beat of M.253, play more dramatically using long generous strokes.

MEASURE 255-258 Play this phrase similarly to the preceding. On the arpeggio (M.258) play lyrically, letting the top A sing long.

MEASURE 259-264 Move forward through to M.263. On the third beat of this measure, play the F sharp—F natural long, almost hysterically. Stop after the first beat of M. 264, and play the run in tempo, especially taking care not to rush the triplets.

MEASURE 267-269 Finish the run evenly, in tempo, stopping on the 16th-note D. Play the last four notes leading into the 16th-note F sharp a little more deliberately. Start a new phrase on the next F sharp, still maintaining an even tempo until the last six 32nd-notes where there is a slight accellerando. The last phrase of this measure is very dramatic in character. At M.269, move forward; at M.270, start to pull out the second eighth-notes of beats one and two, each a real cry, especially the second one. Play beat three in tempo, and pull back on beat four, holding onto the B flat with a feeling of tenuto.

MEASURE 271 Start this phrase deliberately, holding long to the A natural, then move in tempo but with no feeling of rushing.

MEASURE 322 The shift from the octaves D—F feels like a small distance, the F—B flat a large distance. (In this second shift, the thumb becomes an obstacle, making the distance seem greater.)

MEASURE 429 In this passage, use the bow space very compactly; there is a tendency for this type of figure to spread out, thus losing momentum and also for the sound to lose intensity.

MEASURE 440 To maintain the rhythmic equilibrium of this passage and also the equilibrium of the string crossings, take care to play the repeated notes (the first note of each group of 16ths) well.

MEASURE 493 There is no need to play the topline strongly except for the high D.

MEASURE 498 Play the chord first with a solid note F, down bow, then play the harmonic with an upstroke.

rinfz.
Poco a poco affrettando il tempo
e poco a poco crescendo
Poco allargando
Molto moderato
poco cresc.
rinfz.
poco affretando il tempo
poco a poco cresc.

266
267
poco cresc.
268
ten.
poco riten.
Pesante, ravvivando
269
poco riten.
ten.
7 Allegro moderato
272
crescendo molto
274
Basoon
poco f
280
286
poco f
293
poco f
299
piu f

8
304
p subito
sfz
p
310
rfz
mf

313
f
f

316
f
f
f
f
f

319
f
f
322
9
18
ff
343
18
19
20
21
22
23
24
Ob.
Clar.

367
p dolce
f
373
380
f
affettuoso

dim.
p dolce
dim.
pp
poco al poco
string. al
cresc.
poco f
Allegro molto vivace
11
piu
f
piu
decresc.
mp

448

451
cresc.

454
f

458
f

463
fz

468
f
fz

475
f

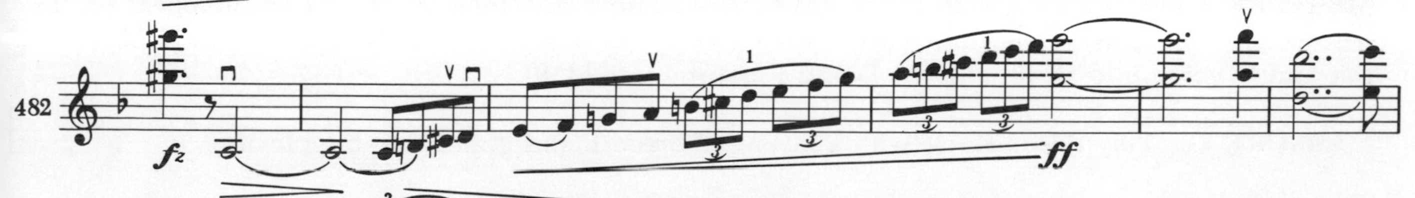
482
fz
ff

488
con tutta forza

494
fz

SECOND MOVEMENT

The continuity of sound in this movement is achieved by playing each note to the very end, as if reluctant to leave it but compelled to move on. The bow action is slow and sustained with a feeling of "breathing" on the second part of each stroke. The mind supplies an up-beat (a psychological up-beat) before each bow change enabling the player to equalize the speed and weight of the stroke both in moving toward the change and moving out of it; thus intensity is maintained and also a feeling of moving forward with great continuity.

MEASURE 6 The accent on the E flat is mainly one of an expressive vibrato, the bow leaning into the string slightly deeper.

MEASURE 9-13 Hold the B flat long, then play the E natural with the vibrato "ready to go". In this phrase, the vibrato should continue from note to note with the same speed and width to maintain the intensity. The triplets in M.11 are slow and deliberate; hold "long" to the second note of each triplet to maintain rhythmic evenness. In M.12, play the grace-note deliberately. Play out very expressively on the second half of M.13.

MEASURE 15 Create another color in this phrase, intimate and subjective in character; use a pressing finger action, raising each very deliberately, the bow action "contained".

MEASURE 18 Play very expressively. Hold the second and fourth 16th-notes "long" so that there is a great feeling of rhythmic evenness and no sense of rushing.

MEASURE 19 Play the grace-note deliberately on the beat.

MEASURE 21-23 Use a flautato stroke continuing the sense of flow in the whole arm, the separations almost unnoticeable. The echo in M.22 is played with a smaller more contained stroke, slowing up on the last 16ths. On the notes leading into M.23, hesitate slightly on the last two notes, playing these with a great melancholy and depth, supporting the sound with a tightening of the diaphragm. To complete the phrase, raise fingers very deliberately, the bow action slow and constant.

MEASURE 32-36 Preserve the rhythmic accuracy of the top melodic line, taking care to give full value to the final 8th-note of each stroke. The bow action should be very connected on both strings. Hold long (to its full value) to the F flat in M.33. The 8th-notes in M.35 must be even, deliberate—no compromise. In M.36, count in 8th-notes so that the 16ths are played very accurately in rhythm.

MEASURE 37-40 Play the high E flat and G very expressively, then let the sound disappear on the descending line. In M.38, the high A and C are similarly expressive as are the A and B flat in M.39, the B flat and D going into M.40, and the D and F natural into M.40.

MEASURE 41 Play this measure with a feeling of breadth and grandeur—big playing.

II.

Adagio di molto ♪=72-80
Clar.
Gp.
Ob.
Fl.
Clar.
Horns
sonoro ed espress.
cresc. poco a poco
ten.
Violins
meno f
cresc.
poco accel.

MEASURE 42 Play the second note of each group very expressively. In order to maintain a sense of line from one group to the next throughout this measure, do not cut the last notes— hold them out to full value.

MEASURE 43 Play the note first before starting to trill. In M.45, hold the first two 16ths of each beat a little longer. Play the last two 16ths piano, very melancholy.

MEASURE 46 The second notes of each group are played expressively, again with no cuts after the last note of each.

MEASURE 47 Make a decrescendo on the first beat. The second and third beats are very intimate, introspective in character, in piano, but with intensity; then begin to play more warmly.

MEASURE 49-52 The flute line is staccato in character; the violin line is legato, sweet, with no roughness in the string crossings. Use a small bow space, accomplishing the crossings with the whole arm, no wrist movement.

MEASURE 53 Every note should receive its full value to achieve a breadth of line; take care not to cut the last note of each group.

MEASURE 55 The grace-note is deliberate in character and should be played on the beat.

MEASURE 62 There should be a feeling of an endless bow in this phrase. Take care of all connections, going into and out of each change of stroke with equal speed and weight, and playing each note as if reluctant to leave it.

MEASURE 65-67 Play the E flat—F—G flat very expressively. The grace-notes in the following measures are deliberate in character. In M.67, hold the D as long as possible before moving up to the harmonic.

3
42
cresc.

45
rinfz.

48
pp sempre
50

51

52

4
53
cresc.
55
tutta forza
dim.

58
dolce
Horn
espr.

63
dim.

THIRD MOVEMENT

This movement suggests the character of a Hungarian dance in its use of dotted rhythms. It demands of the player a judicious control of short-note-leading- to-long—an action which tends to sound labored unless the bow spaces are kept small.

MEASURE 5 On the dotted 16ths be careful not to use a lot of bow, especially the one on the fourth beat. By taking care of this fourth beat whenever it occurs, the player can maintain a better feeling of balance in bow distribution.

MEASURE 36 Initiate the run with a pinch in the bow. On the last two notes of each beat raise the finger very fast for clarity of articulation.

MEASURE 39 Play out more on the lower strings of the octave passage, keeping the shifts light. Maintain a firm line in the wrist when playing octaves.

MEASURE 65 On the fz, jerk the bow, then cut the stroke.

MEASURE 69 These double-stops are sustained in character, the bow playing deep into the string. On the double G, play the harmonic with a "thick", a substantial, fourth finger; the first finger is "thinly" placed.

MEASURE 72-73 On the consecutive down-bow chords, release the pressure of the fingers for each chord. The distance from the high C to the D is large; there is almost no move between the A—B flat. In M.73, initiate each stroke with an accent, being careful not to rush these.

MEASURE 79 Play each chord with a long bow space, returning very fast to prepare for the next.

MEASURE 119 To shorten the length of the glissando, take two single bows on the third and fourth 16ths of the first beat, starting the glissando on the second beat.

MEASURE 175-181 Play the high A expressively. The grace-notes should be played substantially and expressively for each of the trilled notes.

MEASURE 181-187 Play the second note "long" of each slur in this passage.

MEASURE 197 Play the chords two and two (C sharp—G, B—E) instead of the three-note chords indicated.

MEASURE 210-213 Use a spiccato stroke through M.213, then play on the string.

MEASURE 217 Initiate a faster tempo on this measure, and maintain this new tempo strictly until M. 229 where a more deliberate tempo is established. At M.235, begin to slow down.

MEASURE 237 Maintain a sustained character, holding long to the double-dotted quarter notes with big strokes and with no feeling of rushing.

MEASURE 252 Use very long strokes on the chords, recovering very quickly from the first to prepare for the second.

MEASURE 261 In these four measures create a picture of a storm, wild and destructive; surge forward, crescendoing as much as possible, and hold long to the top notes.

MEASURE 267 Move closer toward the bridge to attain as intense a sound as possible.

III

Allegro, ma non troppo ♩=88-92
Va.
poco f
energico
poco f
cresc.
f
mf
cresc. poco a poco
rinfz.
f
fz
mf
ten.
cresc.
rinfz.
f
f
mf
cresc.
poco
a

38
poco
al
ten.
41
1st Violins (2nd time)
pizz.

62
mf
fz

68
mf

74

78
ten.
piu f

83

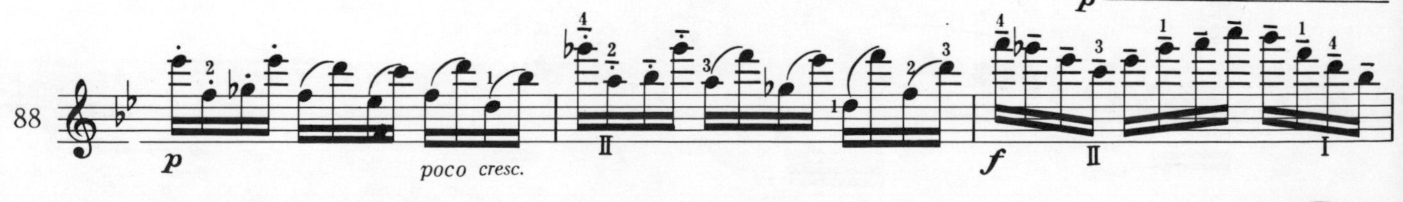
88
poco cresc.

91
cresc. poco a poco

94
Clar.
Bn

100
mf
cresc. poco a poco

103

106

109

112

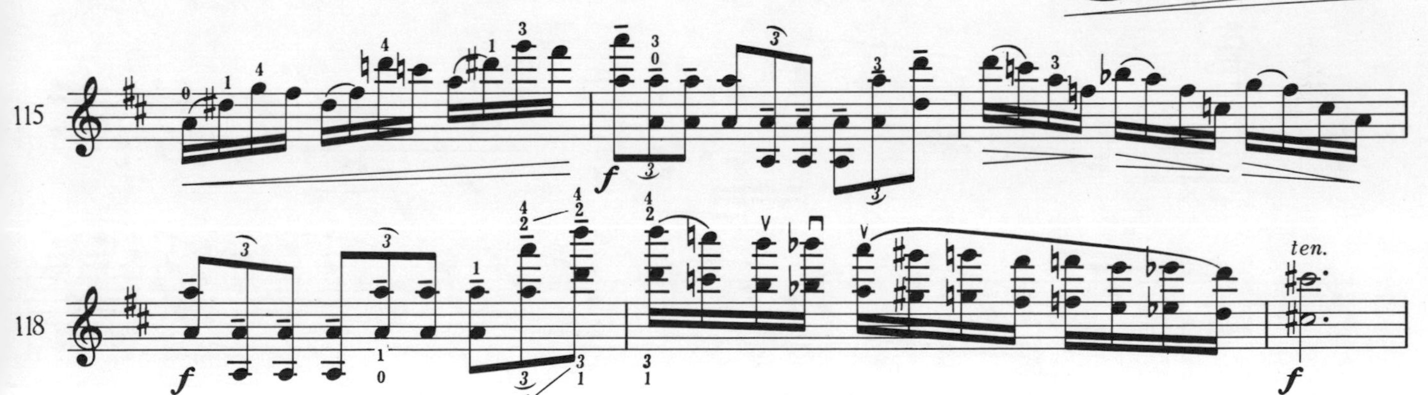
115
f
118
f
ten.
f

121
mf
cresc.

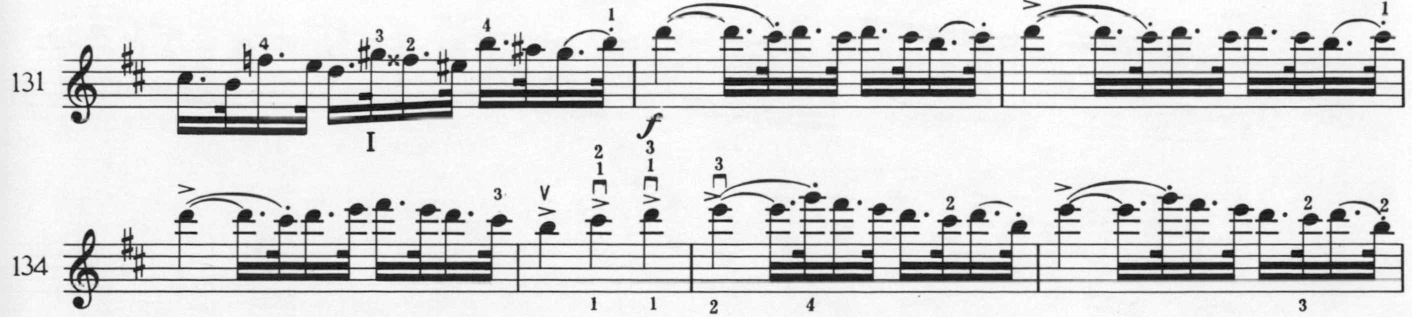
131
f
134

138
mf
142
cresc. poco
144
146
rinfz.
7
fz
150
mf
153
rinfz
ten
mf
156
cresc.
poco
a
poco
al
158
Va.
mf
cresc.
162
164
8
clar.

174
dim.

182

affettuoso
188
energico
193
poco

199

204
209
poco

212
poco

215
cresc.
cresc.

218

crescendo
poco p
cresc. poco a poco
rinfz. poco allarg.
pizz
arco.
sim.
cresc.
pesante
Horns
Trumpet
crescendo possible

TCHAIKOWSKY CONCERTO IN D MAJOR, OP. 35

INTRODUCTION

The Tchaikowsky Concerto is one of the most perfect examples of Romanticism in the violin literature. Its roots lie in that period when all the arts in Russia were flourishing. The whole content of the concerto, although symphonic in much of its character, is a great lyrical song, even within the technical passages, which expresses the great poetic nostalgia and the sadness of pre-revolutionary Russia. The heroicism in the symphonic passages, the lyricism expressed in the ballet-like sections, and the tremendous dramaticism of the whole work are all expressed within traditional classical forms. With all its national characteristics the concerto is really international in its Romanticism, but this Romanticism must be presented through a disciplined approach of maintaining an equilibrium within the phrases and throughout the work.

FIRST MOVEMENT

M.23-25 The orchestra plays F—B flat—G sharp—A and the solo enters as a continuous line with no break or separation; with these last four notes the orchestra asks a question and the solo continues it with the A—B flat. There should be a slight hesitation on the first finger A, before lowering the second. On the B flat there is a slight diminuendo, and it should be played as if it were to suspend the question. The next notes, A—C sharp—E, are played with a deeper bow and more deliberate finger action, with no anticipation of the next note. When crossing strings from E to G hold the E "long;" this is to keep from rushing the crossing and should not distort the rhythm. Play these next two measures singing but with no nuances or color; use a big vibrato and be sure the connections at the tip of the bow are solid. In general, as is the case here, when playing a melodic line conserve the bow space so the sound can breathe at the tip.

M.26-27 The phrase has a feeling of moving forward up to the C sharp of M.26. Then the bow must create a new character: while holding back a little, play flautato and piano from the D to the A in M.27. In the middle of the A create yet another face as a preparation for the next drama. Play more into the string and from G sharp to B each note must slow a little and increase in intensity. Play the A—A sharp—B with a deliberate finger action and not feeling of anticipation. The last A should be thought of as divided into four 16th notes. On each successive 16th make a diminuendo, allargando, and decrease the vibrato proportionately; the bow pressure should die away to nothing. In the shift to the G the bow must continue to move but with no pressure. After the G stop the bow, and the concerto begins in the next measure. This introduction is a perfect example of fragmentation and how detached playing creates attached phrases.

To ADOLF BRODSKY

CONCERTO

VIOLIN

I.

Edited by
Raphael Bronstein

PETER TCHAIKOVSKY, Op. 35
(1840 – 1893)

M.28 The string crossing from A to F sharp should be made with a fast vertical motion of the whole arm; the F sharp should not be too long, like asking a question. The second F sharp, however, must breathe and have a continuous feeling. The 16th notes must be very even; to give rhythmic justice to the open string, the D should be held "long," then, to articulate the next note, raise the second finger high and lower faster. When a finger is skipped between two notes, as with the F sharp—A, the first note must be held longer and the finger for the second note raised high and lowered faster, to insure rhythmic evenness.

M.30-31 The B—G is the same character as the A—F sharp of M.28. Play with a fast string crossing and the G must not be too long. Generally, when playing two notes with the second and third fingers, because there is an inherent interdependence between these two fingers, the first note must be held "longer" and the finger for the second note lowered faster. In M.30 this occurs between the C sharp—D. Be sure to finish the E (hold to its full value) and prepare the first finger for the A, this note must sing with vibrato immediately.

M.32-33 Generally, a shorter note should lead to a longer, here in M.32 the G should lean towards the A; the same is true for M.33, this time, however, the A is even more important because it is the second time this motive occurs.

M.35-37 In M.35 the string crossing from B to C should be made with a very fast vertical motion of the arm. Beginning at M.37 the 8th notes should sing with an intense vibrato and the second notes must be cut short. First give expression on the 8th notes and then cut the 16ths; keep the bow on the string at the tip after the short notes. The drama in this phrase is created with a fast finger action.

M.39-40 In approaching the triplets make a diminuendo and shorten the bow space. The first B flat of the triplets should be held a little longer, and the following notes should be played with a clear even finger motion. Crescendo on the chromatic scale in M.40 and watch that the note before each shift is held longer and the shift is light and fast. On the last four notes broaden out and crescendo.

M.41-45 In M.41 the chords should be played with a slow deep string crossing to create an organ-like sound; play the bottom two notes first, then hold out the top two. When shifting to the A harmonic be sure that the preceding F sharp is held to it full value. Generally, as in M.42, when playing triplets take care that the second note of the three is slower so that all the notes sound even. In M.43 the last E must be held "long" to connect with the next measure. In M.44 hold the B so that there is no anticipation of the shift, and in M.45 prepare the A before playing it; be sure to vibrate immediately.

M.47-49 The character here is orchestral. The bow action must be controlled, raise it slightly at the frog but not at the tip. The string crossings are fast and made with a vertical arm motion. At M.49 the orchestral mood changes to a more lyrical one: use less bow. Each 8th notes must be more expressive and the 16ths should cut short as before. Raise the fingers high and lower faster to insure clear articulation.

M.50-52 In M.50 there is a change of mood, the character becomes more lyrical. The long notes should be played smoothly but not too deep, and the last A in M.50 should be slow and beautiful to serve as an upbeat to M.51. Here the triplets should lead to the long notes. In M.52 the A is played in rhythm, not as in the previous phrase.

M.54-55 The first note in each group of six should be emphasized, not rushed, to give rhythmic stability to the group. Be careful that the third finger in M.54, on D, and in M.55, on G, is played low as the natural tendency is to make these notes too sharp.

M.63-64 The first E is played long, use the whole bow on this note and play the rest at the tip.

M.67-68 In this ascending passage there are two points of rest: the first is on the second A, the phrase then moves up to the F, making a slight accelerando in the 16th notes. To create a tranquil mood on the second half of the F make a poco ritenuto, and diminuendo on the F sharp, then hesitate with the bow before playing the first note of M.69.

Ben sostenuto il tempo

cresc.

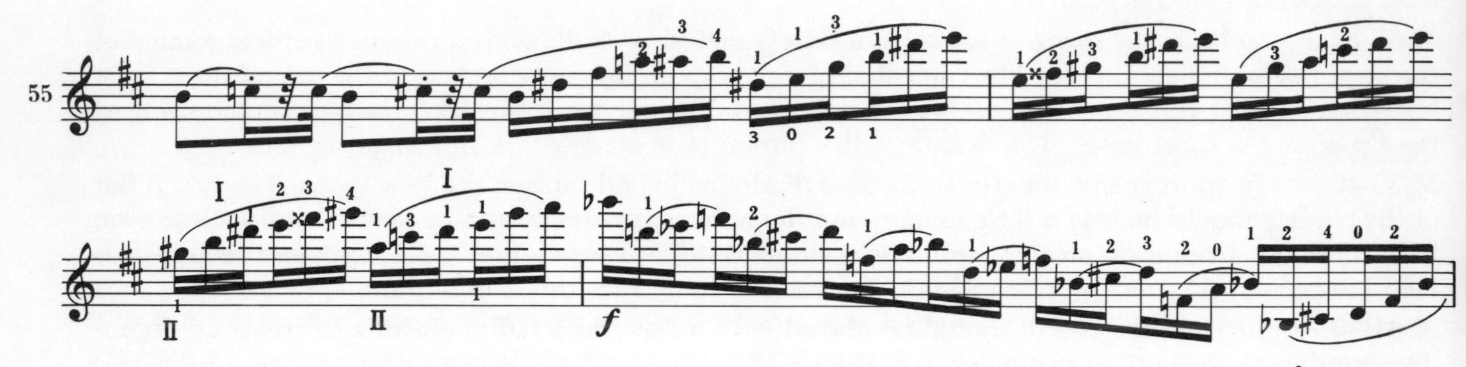

B
cresc.

p.t.

M.69-74 To create the lyrical quality of this phrase play the second quarters longer and more beautiful, and the 16th notes must breathe; to do this prolong the G sharp a little so that the B is not rushed. The same is true each time this figure occurs. In M.71 sing on the B and the F sharp should be felt as the upbeat to the next measure. In M.72 the mood is very melancholic; play the F—E flautato with the whole arm. To make the last B and F sharp very expressive play deeper with the bow and lean into the next measure. In M.73-74 be sure the notes before the shifts are played long with a good vibrato. To be sure the duples are not rushed by the triplets hold out the B sharp—C sharp in M.73 and the D sharp—E in M.74. Play evenly with no ritard in M.74. The character is almost casual and any rubato in this measure will diminish the importance of the theme to follow. To create a melancholic mood play the last three notes flautato.

M.77-80 In M.77 and 78 each of the last notes, F sharp and E, should be played long as upbeats to the next measure. In M.79 play the second note of each triplet longer to insure evenness of rhythm. In M. 80, as in M.74, any rubato will detract from the theme to follow.

M.83-86 On the last F sharp in M.83 stop the bow and hesitate, then move in tempo in M.84. Start this measure with a small bow; when the same note is repeated, as the F sharp, the second time must be played more expressively. The B in M.84 should be expressive and not rushed, play piano in the middle of the bow. To make each successive group of the sequence more dramatic start with a small bow and gradually grow using more space. In M.86 make a crescendo.

M.92-94 The last three notes of each measure should be played deliberately and must give the feeling of leading to the next measure.

M.97 Cut the first note, A, short and go right into the scale in tempo so that there is time to articulate the end of the run. Save the bow in the beginning and spread more at the end so that the sound is even. The last two notes, D—E, should be played stubbornly as they set the tempo for the orchestral entrance. In a passage such as this involving long fast runs subdivide the run into two groups and use the first note of the second group as an anchor. Here you could use the open A as the beginning of the second group.

M.99 The last A natural of this measure must be played low as there is a tendency for all violinists to play it too sharp.

M.101 Play the tremolos with a firm wrist.

M.103 Don't play with any martelé, just push the bow fast with a slight accent on the up-bow stroke. The arpeggio in the second half of the measure is like an answer to the first half; it should be played clearly. Articulate the last three notes well so that the end does not sound rushed.

M.105-106 In M.105 in each group of five notes the first two should be played very fast, and the up-bow accentuated. In M.106 the intonation problems are complex because of the extensions. In general the first group of six notes should feel small in the hand and the second should feel large; the third group is again small. The F sharp should be played low because a whole step between the third and fourth finger is a small distance. In the second group aim high for the B because two whole steps between the first and third fingers is a large distance. The D sharp should be low because the G sharp has a tendency to pull the hand forward and so the next note must be lower to compensate. The E must be lower after the G sharp.

M.110 To maintain control of the rhythm accentuate the upbeat (fourth 16th) of each group.

M.113-117 The bow strokes should be made with a compact forearm motion in the middle of the bow using flat hair. To maintain an even rhythm in the arpeggios think of the ascending arpeggios as answers to the descending, don't rush the answer.

M.119 Start with a small bow and gradually get bigger with the crescendo.

M.123-124 Play the first B sharp a little longer and the next eleven notes faster to compensate. Do the same in the second half on the A. In M.124 the rhythm is even.

M.160 As a general rule short notes always lead to the long, the 8th note, B, is the important note so the shorter preceding notes should lean towards it.

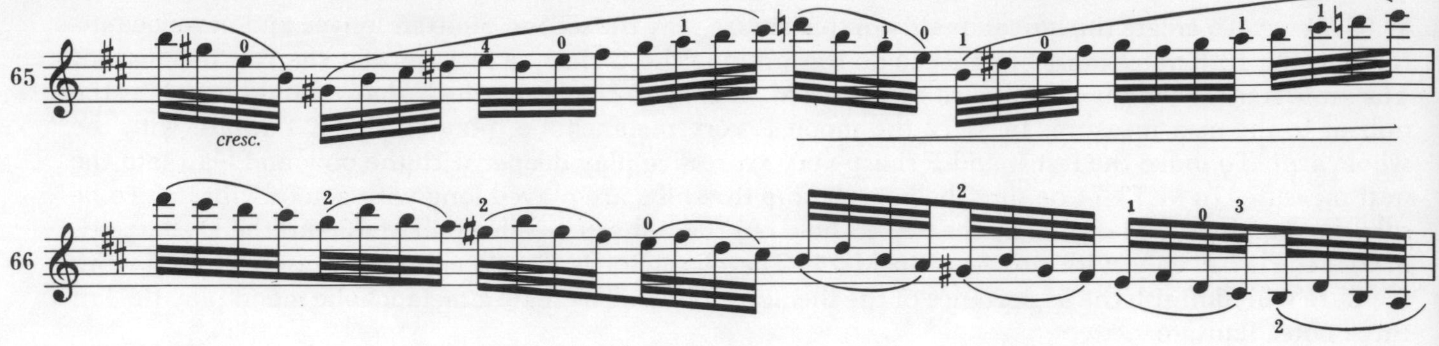
65
cresc.
66

67
poco rit. dim.
p con molto espressione

71

74
mp
poco cresc.

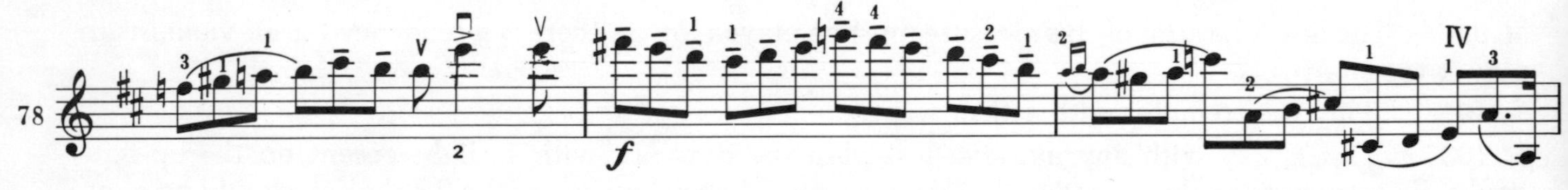
78
f

C
81
mf
p

85
poco
cresc.

88
f

91

94
97
ff
99
mf
crescendo

100

D
101
f

103

105

(Poco) più mosso
f detachè

108
mf

Poco più lento
111

114
f
III

restez

117
restez
III

E (poco) più mosso
ff
mf
I

122
p

124

125
ff
I
II
Moderato assai
126
I
13
F
19

M.162-165 Between M.162-165 the first doublestop of each measure must be longer and the following three notes very even and off the string. Then lean on the first 16th of the next beat to bring out the theme.

M.166 Use a bigger bow on the C natural and play towards the tip, then play the B—A legato and raise the bow. Attack the chords from above by dropping the bow.

M.170 At the end of the run make a slight ritenuto going back into the theme.

M.177-187 The spacial distribution of the bow is very important in this section. Play with a brush stroke and be sure all the notes use an equal, even amount of bow space. Because of the natural gravitational pull downward on the bow arm, push the bow faster with more energy on the up-bows to compensate. Play the single notes clearly especially on the up-strokes and keep the bow arm back so that the bow travels in a straight line, perpendicular to the strings.

M.206 On these chords use a long bow with a heavy feeling and a fast rebound in the arm. The last chord should be held longer than the others and played broken. Play the bottom two notes then make a fast string crossing and play the top two.

M.210 The first chord is long, the following three are fast and short, and the fifth is held. On the last chord of the measure play the top two notes as harmonics and hold them out.

C2 The first chord is broken, first play the two bottom notes then the top two. Slide to the top two notes and hold them, then stop. Each of the following groups of notes should be played more deliberately and within each group lean towards the second note. Connect the last G sharp to the chord without raising the bow and play the chord short.

C3 Hold the first A long and play the arpeggio very fast. The G sharp—A is subito piano. Within the groups of two note slurs be sure the second notes are held out and on each group of notes slow up and diminuendo. Disappear on the last one and play the chord pizzicato: with the index finger play each string individually starting with the G over the finger-board, and on each successively higher string move the hand closer to the bridge.

C4 Hold the first A and the first time play all the notes in tempo, then play poco accelerando the second time, then the third time poco allargando. To minimize the sound of having to break the chords maintain the leverage of the elbow by keeping it high.

C5 On the last arpeggio move the bow quickly on the first note toward the tip, and play the remaining notes there. The C sharp and E are played up-bow with a slight separation, each note a little longer; then there is a luftpause and the A is played as a harmonic. The next group (C6) is exactly the same.

C7 The first chord is short and the second longer, broken two and two. Play the doublestop F sharp—A long then move quickly through the arpeggio to the last three notes, F sharp—A—D, which are played at the tip, not staccato but with a smooth legato bow. Don't make a ritard here, the feeling should be one moving forward.

C8 The first chord is fast and the second broken two and two. Move quickly to the G sharp, then don't rush the end. Slow up on the last two 8th notes and stop before playing the last E. Then stop to create a new mood.

C9 The first E should be played very quietly, then place the bow and fingers quickly for the next note, but play calmly, uninfluenced by the quick chance. Within each group of three notes lean towards the second and on each group play proportionately faster and deeper.

C11 The first two chords are down-bow and long. Then lean the stick towards the bridge by sinking the wrist and concentrate the weight on the bottom two strings, playing at the frog.

C12 Make a diminuendo in proportion and stop the trill on the E then play the grace notes fast moving to the F. Play the F with a light stroke using half the bow. These next notes should be created as three faces: the first is the B flat, the second is G—D flat, and the third is D flat—E. Each face must be detached from the previous and create a different character. On the B flat use a large bow, on G—D flat use a small bow with a quick motion, then hesitate on the D flat and slide to the E. The 16ths should be created with a singing quality.

C13 To create a lyrical line the first G must be warm. Play the chord as an arpeggio and the top F should sing. Then continue by playing the following 16ths lyrically.

Solo
160

molto sostenuto il tempo, moderatissimo
mf
162

164

166

168

170
dim.
mf

172

175
cresc.

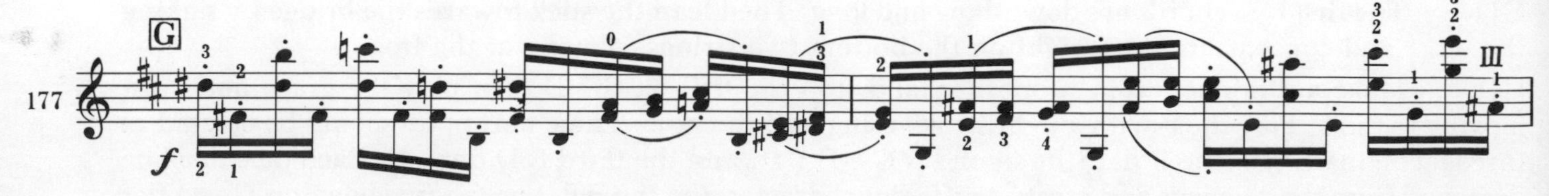
G
177
III

II
179
III

C14 The chord C—A—F sharp is broken; first play the bottom note then the top two. On the next chord, B—G—G, play the B first, then raise the first finger and play the two G's as a fingered octave.

C15 The first chord is broken two and two. To play the chord after the 16th notes raise the bow and drop it on the strings; this happens three times. Then play the next notes at thc tip with the bow on the strings.

M.212 Delay the trill to phrase with the flute in the orchestra.

M.214-216 The string crossing from the low to the high D should be slow and smooth; make the G and F sharp very expressive notes. In M.216 the G should be held before going on to the A.

M.223 Play tenuto on the first F sharp so that it sings.

M.225-228 Care should be taken that this section is not rushed. From 225-227 the playing should be very expressive, watch that the last 16th notes connect well to the first note of the next measure. In M.227 the 16ths are played more melancholic and a bit slower, then in M.228 in tempo again.

M.232-233 In M.232 the C is played deeply with emotion. The mood changes and in M.233 the character becomes light and elegant.

M.250 Hold the B "long" before the shift.

M.251 Make a poco ritenuto.

M.261 The last A prepares the mood for M.262. Play it beautifully so that the new character is quiet and sweet. Be sure that second notes are not rushed, and when a note is repeated, as the G sharp, the second time it should be played more importantly than the first.

M.303 Begin slowly and accelerando so that the last quarter is in tempo.

M.310 From F sharp to A is a small distance. Because of the resistance of the thumb A to D is a big distance.

M.326 To create a dramatic and expressive character play slightly detached.

M.336 Play in the lower part of the bow without rushing. Use a big spiccato with long strokes and on the last quarter hold the top note long.

181
182
184
cresc.
186
16
H
204
ff
17
18
1
208
Cadenza
ff
legato
C3
p
pizz.
mf
arco
C4
cresc.
C5
II
mf
C6
ten
II

C7
ten.
C9
C10
cresc.
C11
Quasi andante
dim.
C12
poco a poco
cresc.
C15
e accelerando
meno mosso
C15
ff
C16
C17
ten.
poco a poco tempo
C18

Tempo primo. Moderato assai
212
p
dolce
cresc.

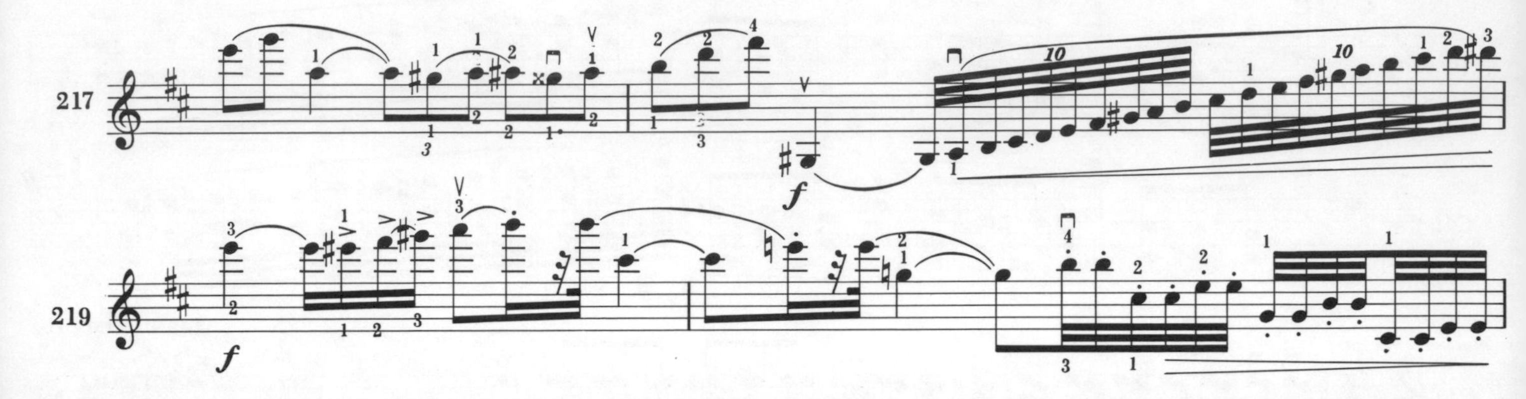
217
f
219
f

221
molto cresc.

222
ff
J
223
mf
cresc.

227
p

230

Ben sostenuto
232
p
grazioso

234

236
cresc.
237
II
239
f
240
II

K
242
f

244
II
cresc.
I
II
II

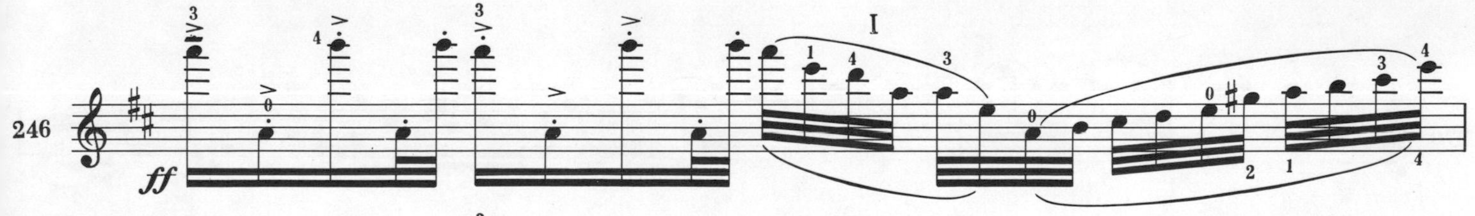
246
ff
I

247
f

248
crescendo
II

249
ff
I

IV
250
mp molto espr.
poco rit.

III
253
III
III

257
p
cresc.

261
p

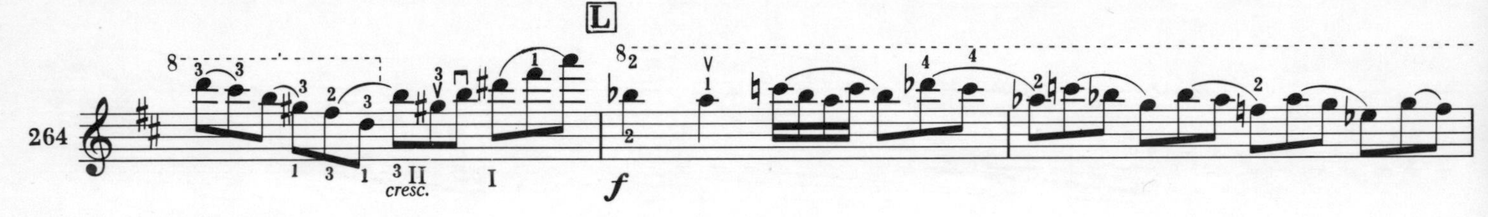
L
264
II
I
cresc.
f

267

270

I
273
ff

II
275
mf
crescendo
I
276

M
277
ff

279

281

(Poco) piũ mosso
282
f
detached

284
mf

285

Poco piũ lento
287
poco
cresc.

288

290

291

293
III

294
N
ff (poco) più mosso

299
p
cresc.

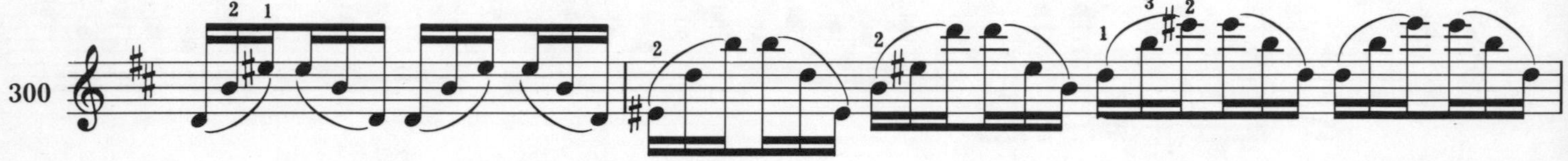
300

302
I

Allegro giusto
303
fp
III
cresc.
II

305
f
restez

307
restez
restez

309
II
311

313

315
O
Stringendo

316
cresc.

318

320
poco acceler.

Piu mosso
323

325

328

331

334

SECOND MOVEMENT

This movement, using elements from Russian folk music, is particularly nationalistic in its character. It reflects the nostalgia and melancholy which marked the end of the Romantic period.

M.13 To give the phrase a melancholy character think of the A as divided into two parts, on the second half lighten the bow pressure and play piano. Take care to rush into the shift to the B flat.

M.14 The last D is played flautato and dryly with no vibrato; it should be as a separate note. In M.15 delay the trill. Special care must be taken when using the fourth finger; because it is generally weaker than the others, hold the note longer and raise the finger faster. Because the F uses the fourth finger, play with substance so that the note speaks well and don't rush it so that the F and E flat are even.

M.18 Play very simply with no anticipation or accents; the bow should be almost flautato. In M.19 play with a smooth bow, very simply and evenly with no extra emotion and sing beautifully.

M.31 To prepare for the tranquility in M.32 the last three 8th notes, which are upbeats, must not be rushed; play them slow and piano.

M.32-33 Play these measures simply and beautifully. In M.33 the last E and F sharp should be played more deliberately.

M.40 To create the intensity in this phrase give full value to each note, with no feeling of anticipation. The finger action must be glue-like, and each note should be created with great love.

M.43 The last two notes should be played deliberately.

M.49 Make a tenuto on the D flat.

M.54 When changing from the lower to upper E flat the string crossing must be made smoothly with the whole arm.

M.60 After the first note each successive note is played more sustained. On the low E flat use a larger bow space.

M.61-64 In Ms. 61 and 62 have the feeling of moving forward on the first six notes and holding back on the last three. M.63 is played evenly and in M.64 hold the B flat, then play evenly.

M.68 Play the B flat with substance. To create a feeling of tranquility the descending passage should be simple and even.

M.71 The last three D's should seem like a reflection. Play them flautato and piano using a long bow with the whole arm.

M.75 Play very expressively, the last harmonic is pianissimo. Stop before going on to M.76, then play piano and simply.

M.78 This phrase should be played simply with a beautiful singing tone and no changes of color.

M.90-94 In M.90 slow up; the second note of each group of three must be played expressively. M.91 should be played deliberately and the last three notes of M.92 very broad and dramatic. In M.93 make a diminuendo and ritenuto in proportion and in M.94 delay the trill. The trill should be fast and continuous, seeming as if it never were to end; stop it before playing the grace notes, which should be simple and even with no expression.

II.Canzonetta

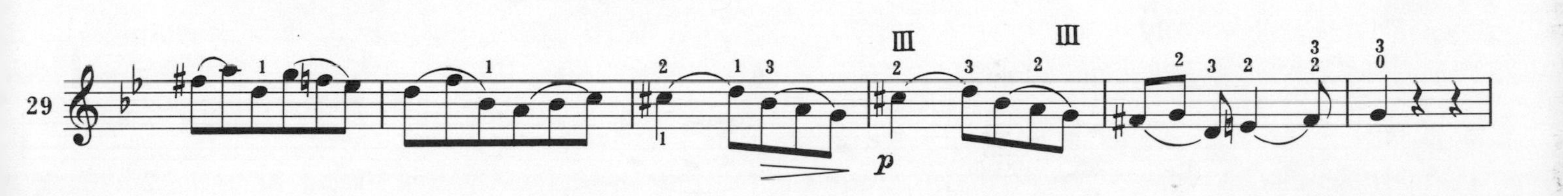

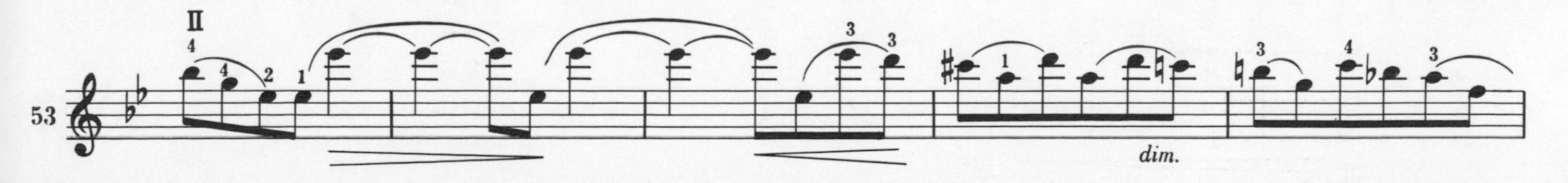

C
espress

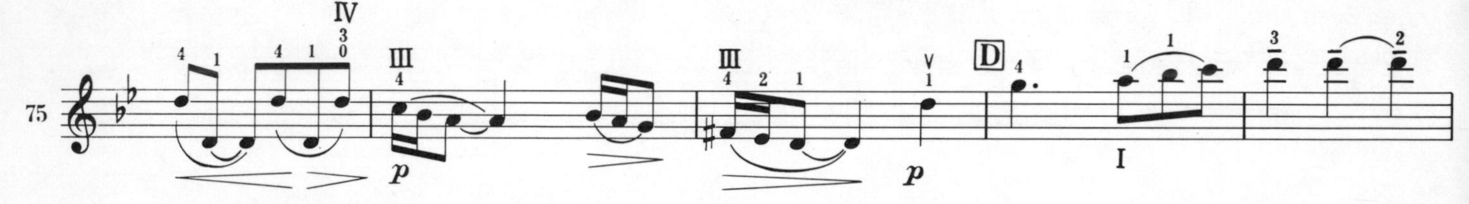
D

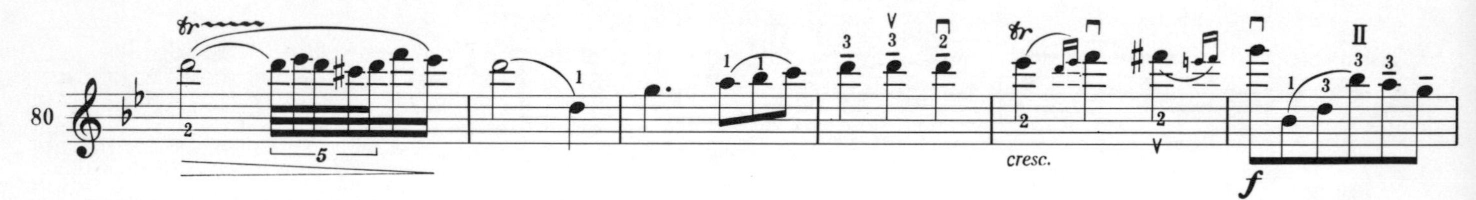
cresc.

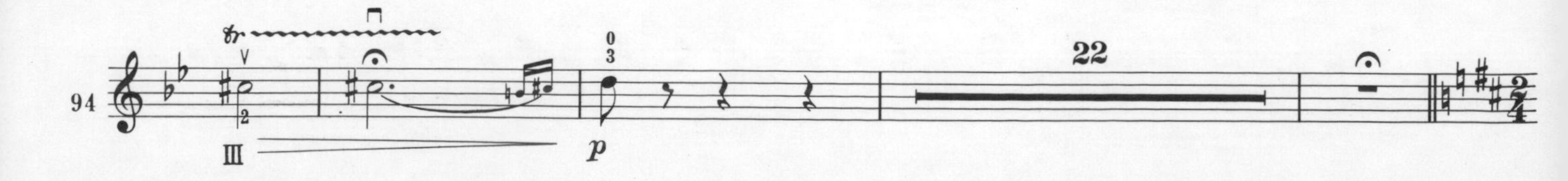

THIRD MOVEMENT

The major portion of this movement should create a picture of galloping Cossack horses. The melodies are typical Russian peasant folk tunes.

M.18 To create the drama of this phrase raise the bow at the tip after the first B flat, play the next three notes, B flat—A—Bflat, more deliberately, and raise the bow after each of the last two notes in the measure. Starting in M.21 accelerate on the chords and play the G sharp short. The last chord should be short and clipped.

M.31 Each time the pizzicato chords occur there should be a feeling of moving forward on each one.

M.37-52 Hesitate before repeating the A. Play M.39 in time and move forward until the C sharp in M.49 where the tempo slows; on each tied note slow the rhythm more.

M.53-54 The first note is played on the string up-bow and should sound connected from the previous note; the D—C sharp—D must be articulated well. In M.54 play the last two notes on the string, then spiccato after that.

M.95-99 Play Ms.95 and 96 stubbornly, then in M.97 make a gradual diminuendo using less bow on each group, working to the tip.

M.144 At the end of the scale slow up to give the new tempo to the orchestra.

M.148-167 This melody portrays a drunken peasant who wants to dance but can't, the playing must be heavy. In M.152 raise the bow on the upper A. In M.158 the melody begins to move but still with heavy playing. Finally in M.160 the peasant dances; play lightly and make a slight accelerando into the tempo primo where the down-bows must be very short.

M.194 Towards the end of the run make a diminuendo and a slight ritard.

M.208 This phrase should be played like a sweet innocent question, with a small bow and singing tone. Both times this phrase occurs the bow should create a smooth legato feeling.

M.216 The character changes here; the playing must be slow and deliberate with a big tone.

M.227 In this measure the mood begins to change. The character in each measure should become sadder and more pathetic, like begging.

M.235 Make a poco a poco accelerando preparing for the tempo primo.

M.294 Play the subito piano with care using a small bow.

M.314 Create a stubborn heavy character by playing with flat hair. All the notes should be double-stops, don't try to play single notes on the bottom.

M.348 Slow up before the poco meno mosso.

M.352 This is a repetition of the drunkard's dance. In M.364 the peasant begins to dance.

M.391-392 In approaching the harmonics slow up. Play them with a soft bow at a 45 degree tilt.

M.393 Play on the string with no staccato. Don't play chopped.

M.416 This melody should be played with a singing tone. The first time it occurs play in tempo and the second time create a more intimate mood. The second time when shifting from C to B prepare the shift by lightening the bow. Hold the C "long" to prepare for the piano on the B and so the shift is not rushed. The third time the melody occurs (M.431) sing more than before.

M.446 Play this broadly and deliberately.

M.559 As before, play all the notes as doublestops on the string.

M.579 Accent the second A sharp.

M.582 The first chord should be long and the G short.

III. Finale

Allegro vivacissimo ♩ = 152

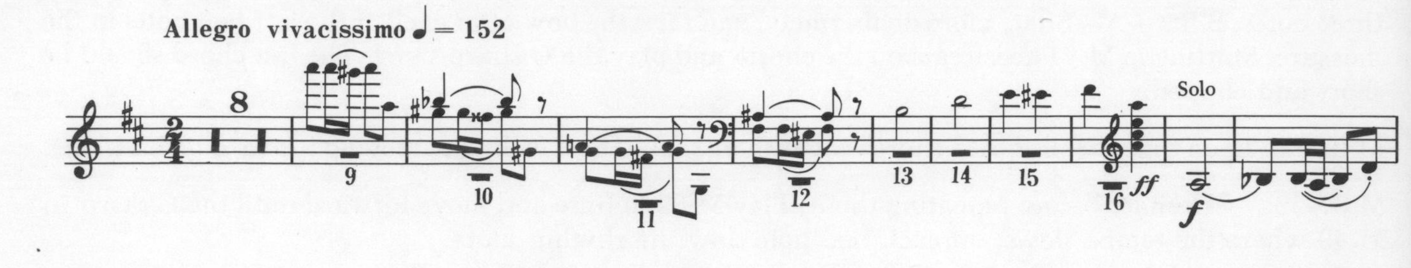

84
cresc.
f

90

96
f
mf
A
p

102
f

108
f

114
8
f
B

120
II
f

127
mf
crescendo

135
dim.

Poco meno mosso
141
8
C
ff

sul G
148
mf
mf

Tempo I
158
p
f

168

176
cresc.

183

188
ff
poco allarg.

Molto meno mosso
D
196
p

213
f

223

Quasi andante
dimin. e rall.
poco a poco accelerando
231
mf

238
sempre stringendo
cresc.
simile

Tempo I
243
p
f

248
dim.
p

253
f
p

258
f
p

263
f
p
f

268
p
mf

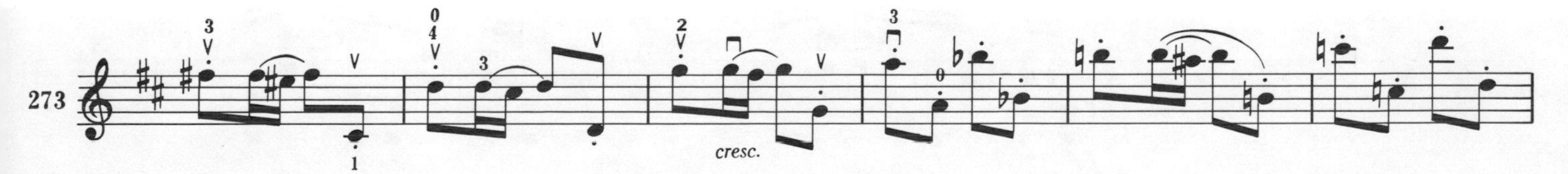
273
cresc.

279
f
E
f

284
III
IV
III
IV

290
p

295

300

305

310
F
f

315

320

325
ff
3

333
p
cresc.
337
f
p
cresc.

cresc.

G
Poco meno mosso
sul G

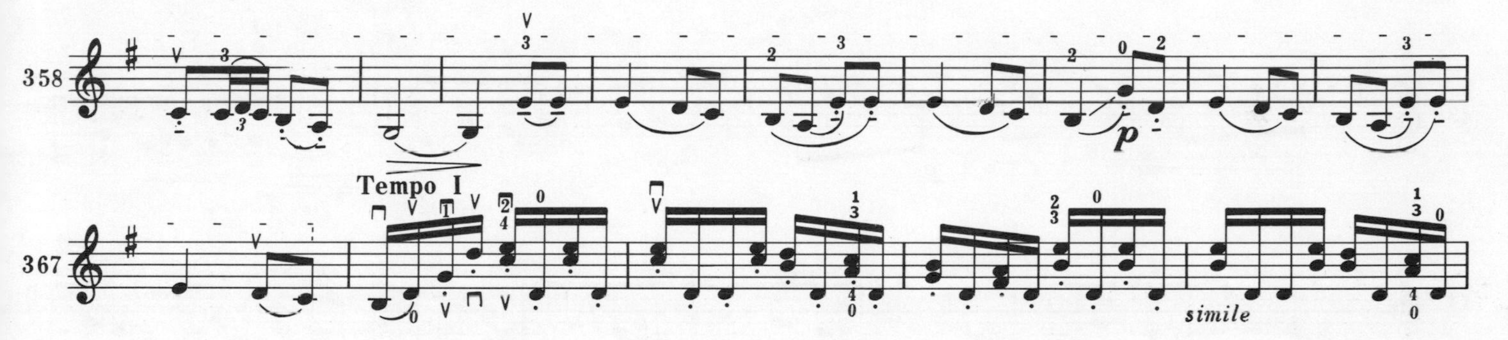
Tempo I
simile

poco meno mosso
rit.

Molto meno mosso
H
poco allarg.

414
sul G
Poco a poco rall.
mf

422

430
Quasi andante
f

438
p

445
pp
cresc.

452
Poco
poco
to Insert
Tempo I.
p

457
f
dim.
p

463
f
p

469
f
p

475
p
f
p

481
mf
cresc.

487

493
f
dim.

500
I
mf

506
f
f

513
K
f

520
II

526
f
mf
cresc.
ff
21

556
L
22
23
24
f

564

571

578

588
p
cresc.
M
f

594
cresc.
sempre ff

600

606

612
Piano

619

626
ff

FROM THE PUBLISHER

The Science of Violin Playing may sound like a presumptuous title. The science of anything signifies in most minds, a complete and total summation of all the present knowledge of the subject. Music is said to be an art and a science. If this be so, and I agree, then the SCIENCE OF VIOLIN PLAYING is just that. This book does not reiterate what others have said or written about, but rather what has not been put down in words.

Art is subjective while science is exact. This book, if followed to the letter, will do exactly what it states: no trial or error. Professor Bronstein does not over-elaborate his statements, consequently the reader should take each statement and let it mellow. It is the scientific approach that has always appealed to the Professor. As a student of Mr. Bronstein two decades ago, I remember very vividly his analogies of the finger board as a chess board, and the bow as a brush, while I was the creator or painter. There was a whole world of circumstances involved with the four fingers. Their weaknesses, strengths and idiosyncrasies were those of real people challenging each other for existence. "Comes the revolution," the Professor would say, "speaking from first hand knowledge, and you knew that all the world's problems lie at your fingertips." This book should give you freedom to create the world that you believe in.

Paul Paradise

ACKNOWLEDGMENTS

I wish to acknowledge my gratitude to Eugene Lowinger and Paul Paradise for their assistance in the preparation of this book and especially Mary Jane Metcalfe whose interest and close collaboration has proved invaluable to me.

Raphael Bronstein

The *Science of Violin Playing* by Raphael Bronstein contains such a plenitude of splendid material that I am pleased to pronounce it a "must" reading for every string player.

Its underlying concept is a plea for creative individuality. Professor Bronstein carefully presents the muscular-psychological problems of technic and interpretation. In his chapter on intonation he advances where others have left off. Of course, the basis of good intonation is hearing the notes in mind before playing them and practicing them until they are well in tune. Bronstein discusses intonation from the physio-psychological viewpoint so that one can develop a very highly flexible, sensitive kinesthetic sense of the fingerboard. Nothing in his presentation is vague. He presents numerous specific exercises to aid in achieving good intonation.

In the chapter on development of practical technic he, after a philosophic explanation, proceeds to present specific exercises which include the muscular interaction of finger motion:

1. with other fingers;
2. the hand;
3. the arm.

He detailedly explains the development of muscles toward accomplishing these aims, with each finger separately treated. He is equally as scientific in his presentation of the development of practical right-hand technic.

In his chapter on interpretation, I am happy to say he points out specific deficiencies in our playing too often overlooked. There is tremendous benefit to be had from his exposition of the subtle details of good musicianship: the technical aspect of interpretation and the spiritual and psychological values. To become absorbed in this material will result in receiving from it inspiration and knowledge.

Samuel Applebaum

TABLE OF CONTENTS

BIOGRAPHICAL NOTES

Raphael Bronstein's teaching career in the United States began in 1923 as an assistant to Leopold Auer. Since then, his reputation and fame as an artist-teacher has grown steadily both here and abroad.

Russian-born, Raphael Bronstein made his debut at the age of ten as soloist with the Warsaw Philharmonic and toured throughout Poland and Russia as a recitalist and soloist with orchestras. He received his early training with Isidor Lotto in Warsaw. He won the scholarship competition offered at the Petrograd (now Leningrad) Conservatory for study in Leopold Auer's class at the age of 12, graduating from there in 1917. During the time he was studying in Petrograd, he was a member of the Glazunov String Quartet, and the Duke of Mecklenburg Quartet, touring with these groups as well as appearing as recitalist and soloist. After his graduation from Auer's class, he toured extensively in Spain and Portugal before coming to the United States.

In addition to his private teaching, Professor Bronstein held the position of musical director (1937-41) for the Society for the Advancement of Young Musicians, which started performing careers for many outstanding young artists. He was also director of the New School of Music from 1939 to 1942. In 1947, he joined the faculty of the Hartt College of Music (now a part of the University of Hartford), a position which he currently holds as visiting professor. He also has taught at Boston University as a visiting professor (1954-1962). He is currently a member of the faculty at Manhattan School of Music, which he joined in 1950, at Mannes College of Music since 1956, and in 1966, he was invited to lecture for the string faculty of the Leningrad Conservatory in Russian and to listen to some of the outstanding students at the Leningrad and Moscow Conservatories.

Professor Bronstein also has been engaged in giving master classes at colleges throughout the country, some of which were: University of Oklahoma, University of Kentucky, Baldwin Wallace College, Ohio, and in 1975 master classes at Northern University of Arizona at Flagstaff. In February 1976 Professor Bronstein was presented the Artist Teacher Award of 1976 by the American String Teachers Association.